D1594244

LONGCHENPA'S
ADVICE *from the*
HEART

© 2008 Shang Shung Institute
Località Podere Nuovissimo
58031 Arcidosso (GR)
Italy
www.shangshunginstitute.org
info@shangshunginstitute.org

Cover and graphics by Daniel Zegunis
Cover photo by Yeshi Silvano Namkhai

ISBN 978-88-7834-102-9
IPC—534EN08—274E
Approved by the International Publications
Committee of the Dzogchen Community
founded by Chögyal Namkhai Norbu

LONGCHENPA'S ADVICE *from the* HEART

CHÖGYAL NAMKHAI NORBU

Transcribed and edited by
ELIO GUARISCO

ཤང་ཞུང་ཡིག་ཆ་བསྡུ་སྒྲིག་ཁང་ལས་བྱུང་།
Shang Shung Edizioni

CONTENTS

FOREWORD   9

INTRODUCTION   11

The Knowledge of Dzogchen—

Base, Path and Fruit   11

The Base—Essence   12

The Base—Nature   12

The Base—Energy   15

The Importance of Transmission   16

Symbolic Transmission   17

Oral Transmission   18

Direct Transmission   18

Devotion and Knowledge

Grounded in Experience   19

Anuyoga—Instantaneous Transformation   20

The Path: the Essence of the Practice   23

The Importance of Guruyoga   25

Guruyoga in Dzogchen   27

The Conduct of a Practitioner   28

Being Present   29

Ordinary Presence and Instant Presence   31

The Ultimate Purification   31

The Awareness of Circumstances   32

Direct Introduction to our Real Nature   33

THIRTY WORDS OF ADVICE

FROM THE HEART   39

Longchenpa's Text   39

Commentary by Chögyal Namkhai Norbu 47
Homage to the Master   47
The Exhortation   48
The First Word of Advice   49
The Second Word of Advice   49
The Third Word of Advice   52
The Fourth Word of Advice   53
The Fifth Word of Advice   55
The Sixth Word of Advice   56
The Seventh Word of Advice   57
The Eighth Word of Advice   60
The Ninth Word of Advice   61
The Tenth Word of Advice   61
The Eleventh Word of Advice   63
The Twelfth Word of Advice   63
The Thirteenth Word of Advice   65
The Fourteenth Word of Advice   67
The Fifteenth Word of Advice   70
The Sixteenth Word of Advice   71
The Seventeenth Word of Advice   73
The Eighteenth Word of Advice   74
The Nineteenth Word of Advice   75
The Twentieth Word of Advice   77
The Twenty-first Word of Advice   79
The Twenty-second Word of Advice   83
The Twenty-third Word of Advice   84
The Twenty-fourth Word of Advice   85
The Twenty-fifth Word of Advice   85
The Twenty-sixth Word of Advice   86
The Twenty-seventh Word of Advice   88

The Twenty-eighth Word of Advice 89
The Twenty-ninth Word of Advice 91
The Thirtieth Word of Advice 94
Concluding Advice 97
How to Integrate the Practice
in Daily Life 97
Index of Tibetan Terms and Names 101
Tibetan Text 107

FOREWORD

THIS BOOK CONTAINS a new translation of Longchenpa's *Thirty Words of Advice from the Heart* (*sNying gtam sun bcu pa*) and the edited transcription of the commentary given by Chögyal Namkhai Norbu during the retreat that took place from November 25th to 29th, 2007 in Barcelona, Spain. I translated Longchenpa's text from Tibetan using two different editions of the original work: one contained in the collected writings of Longchenpa, the other published by Ogyan Kunsang Chökorling, Darjeeling, India.

Longchenpa Trime Öser (1308-1363) was one of the most important Dzogchen masters of Tibet. He is to the Nyingma school what Tsongkhapa is for the Gelug, Sakya Pandita to the Sakya and Marpa Chökyi Lodrö to the Kagyü. His beautiful and inspired words of advice were probably written when Longchenpa was still a young man engaged in his studies.

This master's scriptural learning and realization were equal to those of the famous saints who graced the land of India, and true to his words of advice, his was a disciplined life spent in forest and mountain hermitages. Longchenpa's *Thirty Words of Advice* are like nuggets of gold offered to us in his open hand, so that their inspiration can turn our mind to a sincere and uncorrupted spiritual practice.

With his clear introduction to the principles and practice of Dzogchen, Chögyal Namkhai Norbu sets in context the thirty words of advice and then proceeds to explain each one as the basis of Longchenpa's spiritual experience, in a way that is relevant to us as individuals in our time.

I wish to thank Adriano Clemente, Igor Legati and Maurizio Mingotti for their substantial contributions in editing and annotating the final version of the manuscript, and Nancy Simmons for thoroughly revising the English of the entire book.

Elio Guarisco

INTRODUCTION

The Knowledge of Dzogchen:
Base, Path and Fruit

D ZOGCHEN CONTAINS a very important and comprehensive knowledge of the Base, Path and Fruit.[1] 'Base' refers to the principle of our real condition. 'Path' refers to the way in which we can obtain the realization of that condition. 'Fruit' is the final result of the practice. These three points are shared by all kinds of teachings, not only those of Dzogchen. However, the understanding of what the Base is differs completely in Sutra, Tantra and Dzogchen.[2] For this reason, the practice and the idea of what realization is are different. What is the Base? In Dzogchen the condition of the base is presented as three primordial wisdoms.[3] Although our real nature cannot be fully explained in words, we need to have a general idea, so that through these wisdoms, we can describe at least in an approximate way what our real nature is. 'Three primordial wisdoms' does not mean that these three are separate. However, for didactic purposes we can understand primordial wisdom through its three different aspects: Essence, Nature and Energy.[4]

---

[1]   A three-fold classification used to present the Buddha's teachings: Base or Ground (Tib. *gzhi*), the primordial condition; Path, (*lam*) or the spiritual training that allows one to free oneself from the cycle of existence or saṃsāra, and Fruit (*'bras bu*)—the result or the end of the spiritual path.
[2]   Sūtra (Tib. *mdo*) is the path of renunciation (*spong lam*) embodied in the Hīnayāna and Mahāyāna teachings of the Buddha. Tantra or Vajrayāna is the path of transformation (*sgyur lam*) believed to have been taught by the Buddha is his Saṃbhogakāya form. Dzogchen is the path of self-liberation (*rang grol lam*), first taught in our world by Garab Dorje.
[3]   Tib. *ye shes gsum.*
[4]   Tib. *ngo bo, rang bzhin, thugs rje.*

THE BASE—ESSENCE

Essence is emptiness, the real nature of all things. The Sutras also speak of this principle. The Mahayana Sutras, in particular, emphasize to a great extent emptiness or Shunyata.[5] In this regard, the well known Buddhist term Dharmadhatu, in which *dharma* refers to all things, all existence, and *dhatu* to the real nature, simply means emptiness. Emptiness is the base: it is like space, in which all things can manifest and exist. All sentient beings and their sensory fields exist in and by that space.

The Essence is also explained as the Dharmakaya.[6] Kaya means dimension, in this case the real dimension of all things, which is emptiness—the Dharmadhatu. Here, we must distinguish the term Dharmadhatu from its twin term, Dharmata. We have two different terms because Dharmadhatu is the real nature of all things and beings, all phenomena, while Dharmata represents the ultimate condition of sentient beings only. If we speak of the real condition of a table, for example, we do not say Dharmata but Dharmadhatu.

THE BASE—NATURE

The second aspect of the Base is its Nature, which is clarity. Emptiness, although we cannot see it or identify it as something concrete, possesses an infinite potentiality that manifests as clarity. From emptiness everything pure and impure can manifest and all these manifestations, regardless of their purity or impurity, are part of clarity. Many practitioners understand clarity as the result of a practice done to develop some kind of clairvoyance, or as a manifestation of pure vision. But clarity is actually a very general term, which

---

[5] Emptiness, or Śūnyatā in Sanskrit, is the foundation of the view in the Mahāyanā teaching. Although mentioned in the original Sutras of the Buddha, emptiness was emphasized by Nāgārjuna, the main figure of the Madhyamaka philosophy.

[6] Dhārmakāya (*chos sku*), along with Saṃbhogakāya (*longs sku*) and Nirmāṇakāya (*sprul sku*), is one of the three aspects of the enlightened dimension.

applies to both pure and impure vision. We may see a tree, or even something ugly, and neither is pure vision yet both are part of our clarity.

Let us take for example the symbol of the Tantric teaching, which is the vajra.[7] A vajra has two symmetrical ends. The most commonly seen vajra has five prongs at both ends but there is also another type that is nine-pronged and originated later, when Padmasambhava[8] introduced Vajrayana to Tibet. The nine prongs of this vajra symbolize the nine vehicles[9] which are spoken of in the Dzogchen and Anuyoga traditions.

In both cases, the two symmetrical ends of the vajra symbolize the two aspects of our vision, pure and impure. The central sphere on which both ends are based symbolizes our real nature and how, through the practice of the path, the aggregates of our impure condition[10] can be transformed into pure vision.

Ordinary sentient beings have impure vision because all they experience is related to the potentiality of their karma. At present, as we are human beings, we have this human vision which is distinct from the vision a dog or a bird has. Thus, all sentient beings have their own vision created by the potentiality of their karma. This is what is meant by impure vision, it is a vision dictated by karma.

---

[7] Vajra (Tib. *rdo rje*) is a Sanskrit word meaning both thunderbolt and diamond, used to define the enlightened state that destroys all ignorance and is in itself indestructible. Here it refers in particular to a scepter-like symbolic object used in Vajrayāna or Tantric Buddhism.

[8] Padmasambhava, or Guru Rinpoche as he is more commonly known by Tibetans, was the master from Oḍḍiyāna who introduced Vajrayāna Buddhism to Tibet in the 8th century.

[9] These are the nine vehicles (*theg pa dgu*) taught in the Nyingma school: the worldly vehicle of Gods and Humans; the vehicle of the Śrāvakas and Pratyekabuddhas; the vehicle of the Bodhisattvas; the three outer tantras of Kriyā, Ubhaya and Yoga Tantra; and the three inner tantras of Mahāyoga, Anuyoga and Atiyoga.

[10] Our impure condition is composed of the five aggregates (*phung po lnga*) that constitute the psycho-physical make-up of the person: physical form, sensations, conceptions, volitions, and consciousness.

We also have pure vision, in our potentiality. From the beginning we possess Essence and Nature, and through this Nature the potentiality of the Essence can spring forth. In pure vision, everything manifests through the lights of the five colors. The five colors have the same nature of the five elements, which are the base of our impure vision.

Yet, we do not have pure vision because all our vision is a materialization of the potentiality of our negative karma. For example, although the nature of water is the color white, if we want to quench our thirst, that color by itself won't do; we really need to drink a glass of water on the material plane. This is the way in which our karmic vision unfolds. For that reason, when we practice, at the end we dissolve everything into its real nature and in that way we can enter pure vision.

In the Dzogchen teaching, Essence and Nature are presented as 'primordial purity' and 'self-perfection'.[11] Primordial purity refers to the condition of original purity, not to a purity acquired by cleansing the impure through spiritual practices. This condition, which is pure from the beginning, is emptiness. However, when we fall into the duality of subject and object, we begin to accept 'this' and reject 'that', and following that pattern we accumulate much negative karma.

With the accumulation of the power of negative karma, our impure vision becomes ever denser. Nonetheless, even this thickened, impure vision is, from the beginning, part of our primordial potentiality. Thus, in following the teaching it is very important to understand that our real nature is primordially pure.

Even if we live in impure vision, we know that the impure vision is part of our self-perfected qualification, and in that way we can enter pure vision. While in Tantrism there is the idea of pure and impure vision, and that the impure vision must be transformed into pure vision, in Dzogchen we need only the knowledge or understanding that our real condition is perfect, pri-

---

[11] Tib. *ka dag* and *lhun grub*.

mordially pure and self-perfected, and working with this knowledge we try to enter again and again into our own real nature.

THE BASE—ENERGY

For the third aspect, that of Energy, we must understand that from the beginning energy unfolds and gives rise not only to pure but also to impure vision. In this regard, the cause of all emotions is called ignorance, *marigpa*[12] in Tibetan. *Marigpa* does not refer to what ordinarily we consider ignorance, that is, lack of education. In the Sutras, *marigpa* is considered to be the first of the twelve links of interdependent origination.[13] Everything originates from that ignorance.

What is ignorance in this context? Even if in our condition we possess, from the very beginning, the potentiality of primordial purity and self-perfection, we do not know it and we search for realization outside ourselves. We resemble the person who is searching for the elephant on which he is riding; or, in another simple example, we are like a person who looks for his hat, having forgotten that he is wearing it. Likewise, although we have always possessed the self-perfected state, we are ignorant of this and become totally conditioned by dualistic vision, suffering endlessly in the cycle of transmigration. Thus, the cause of that cycle is *marigpa*.

In the Tibetan language there are two terms, *rigpa* and *marigpa*. *Rigpa* means to have the complete knowledge of our real condition. That is, upon receiving the transmission from a teacher, we apply the methods, and through these we discover what our real nature is. *Marigpa* is the contrary of this, and it is negative, as it implies a lack of knowledge. It is the root of all our ignorance.

[12] Tib. *ma rig pa*, ignorance (of our state), not having knowledge of the primordial state.
[13] The twelve branches, or links, of the dependent arising of phenomena in cyclic existence: i) Ignorance, ii) Volitions, iii) Consciousness, iv) Name and form, v) Six sensespheres, vi) Contact, vii) Feeling, viii) Attachment, ix) Grasping, x) Existence, xi) Birth, xii) Old age and death.

THE IMPORTANCE OF TRANSMISSION

When we approach Dzogchen, the first and most important thing is to know our real condition. Thereafter, we learn many methods and instructions. People say, 'I want to follow Dzogchen'. But how does one become a Dzogchen student? It is not sufficient only to buy a book and read it.

First one must establish a connection with a teacher who has a real knowledge of Dzogchen. The simple fact that a teacher is famous and high ranking does not qualify him or her to be a Dzogchen teacher. Nor is it sufficient that the teacher is very learned and has the title of pandit,[14] or great scholar. It also happens that people try to approach Dzogchen through analysis. They think of Dzogchen as a philosophy and apply themselves to the study of Dzogchen texts. Others consider Dzogchen a religion and follow Dzogchen on the basis of faith. There are indeed many ways of approaching the Dzogchen teaching, but a teacher who does not have a sound knowledge of Dzogchen will never be able to introduce you to the Dzogchen state, so you will not obtain that knowledge. Someone may perform a very interesting and important ceremony or rite. Or, they may teach Dzogchen on the basis of many years of study of the Dzogchen texts, and those who listen may think that it is something fantastic. But that is intellectual learning and one cannot obtain the knowledge of Dzogchen in that way.

A teacher who has real knowledge instructs you orally in the total knowledge of Dzogchen; he does not impart just an intellectual knowledge. The teacher makes you understand that you can discover your real nature through practice. The disciple is not the master and the master is not the disciple. They are two completely different individuals. The teacher may have the knowledge that you don't, and the teacher who has this knowledge and experience of Dzogchen can make you understand what you should do.

---

[14] An Indian title given to scholars learned in the traditional fields of study: grammar, dialectics, medicine, arts, and religious philosophy.

SYMBOLIC TRANSMISSION

There are three kinds of transmission in the Dzogchen teaching—symbolic, oral and direct.[15] The first, the symbolic transmission, is mostly related to our physical reality, to our body which is connected to the material world. In this transmission the teacher, for example, may show us a crystal rock that is clear, limpid, transparent, and explain that our own essence or emptiness is just like that crystal. He may explain that our potentiality manifests when there are certain circumstances, just as the crystal emits rainbow lights all around when it is struck by sunrays or by light. If you look at a crystal rock when the secondary causes are not present you cannot see any lights, but when these causes are present the lights become visible. In this way, the teacher also makes us understand how visions can manifest. That is an example of the symbolic transmission.

Then, for all different kinds of manifestations, the teacher may use the example of the mirror. He may not show an actual mirror, but when he says 'mirror', we have an idea of what a mirror is, because we live in a modern world and we have mirrors everywhere. Regardless of a mirror's shape, when you look into it your face appears there instantly. That is the potentiality of the mirror. Your face appears in the mirror because you are in front of it. That is an example of how all things manifest instantly when the secondary circumstances are present. This is another instance of symbolic transmission.

In Dzogchen, when masters give an introduction, as symbols they use a crystal rock and a peacock feather. The crystal is used as a symbol to introduce primordial purity and the peacock feather as a symbol to introduce the self-perfected potentiality. What does the peacock feather signify? On the feather we can see a circle, or *thigle*. A pictorial representation of the *thigle* and the circle in the peacock feather look similar, yet there is difference, in that the pictorial representation has been painted by someone—it is not natural.

---

[15]   These are usually called: the symbolic transmission of awareness-holders, the oral transmission of individuals, and the direct transmission of enlightened beings.

The self-perfected potentiality of *lhundrub* is present in our real nature from the beginning; it was not developed through the practice. For this reason we use the peacock feather, which symbolizes how all things arise in the course of time as manifestations of energy.

ORAL TRANSMISSION

Oral transmission is related more to our Voice. As you may know, our existence unfolds on the three levels of Body, Voice and Mind.[16] All teachings and methods are related to them. Thus, for example the symbolic transmission is more related to the physical, the Body, the oral transmission is related to the Voice and the direct transmission to the Mind. In the oral transmission the teacher explains the Base, the Path and Fruit[17] and the students, even if they do not discover their real nature at that time, can still listen and gain at least a general understanding.

DIRECT TRANSMISSION

The most important transmission is the direct transmission, which is related to the Mind. Although this is the most important transmission, if one does not work with the symbolic and the oral transmissions, one cannot enter into the direct transmission or direct introduction.

Some people have the idea that the direct transmission is very secret and that if their teacher gives them such a transmission they become realized. This reflects a passive attitude on the part of those students, because they think that by simply receiving the direct introduction from the teacher, they become enlightened. But no teacher can do that, not even Buddha Shakyamuni[18] could. He said, 'I give you the path, but realization depends on you.'

---

[16] Body, Voice (or Speech) and Mind can have an ordinary or an enlightened state. Accordingly they are called, in Tibetan, *lus, ngag, yid* or *sku, gsung, thugs* respectively.
[17] See note I.
[18] The historical Buddha (or 'awakened one'), Siddhārta Gautama prince of the Śākyas, who lived in India approximately 563 to 483 BCE.

He never claimed that the realization of others came from him. If this were possible he would have enlightened all beings!

Thus, it is very important to prepare through the symbolic and the oral transmissions in order to gain very precise knowledge during direct introduction.

When the teacher explains for days and days, he is actually preparing students to receive the direct introduction. Thereafter, the students receive the direct introduction and can discover their real nature, a cause for rejoicing for the teacher as well. Thus, the role of the teacher is to make one understand that the most important thing to succeed in is the discovery of one's real nature.

Devotion and Knowledge Grounded in Experience

Some traditions emphasize to a great extent the need of devotion to the teacher and to the teaching. One can develop one's devotion to the best of one's capability, but it will still be fleeting. One may feel intense devotion today but, after days and years have passed, one's devotion weakens till one feels it no longer. This indicates that one's devotion was artificial and artificial devotion is not the point.

The main point is to listen well to the teacher's instructions and try to do one's best, working with the teacher during direct introduction. When finally we discover our real nature we also really understand the teacher's qualities, the qualities of the teachings and the qualities of the transmission. At that point, even if we want to change our faith, we cannot change it anymore because we have a knowledge which is grounded in experience.

For example, if I show you a golden pen, you see and know that it is a golden pen without having to imagine what the object I am holding in my hands is. If you have not actually seen it, you can just imagine that I was holding such a pen, but if someone claiming to be a friend of mine tells you that I lent him my pen and that it was not a golden one, your idea changes. That is how artificial devotion is. So it is very important to have that approach.

Anuyoga—Instantaneous Transformation

In the Nyingma tradition there is a system of transformation called Anuyoga which is unique as it is not found in the other schools.[19] For example, the Sakya, Kagyü and Gelug tradition consider the Kalachakra Tantra[20] one of the highest tantras, but even this tantra does not belong to Anuyoga.

The Anuyoga system originated in ancient times in Sri Lanka and later developed and spread gradually in a country called Trusha. At a later time, for reasons unknown to us, Anuyoga disappeared in Sri Lanka, where Hinayana Buddhism took hold. In Trusha, Anuyoga developed to a great extent and, later, on the advice of Guru Padmasambhava, some Tibetan translators went to Trusha and translated the Anuyoga texts into the Tibetan language. We know that Trusha is the present Kirghizstan, until recently a Soviet republic. Reports say that in Kirghizstan there are many statues of Bodhisattvas although no one knows why they are found there, in a Muslim country. All the important Anuyoga teachings that developed in Trusha, not only the texts, but also the transmissions and related methods, are now preserved in Tibet. Following

---

[19] The four main schools of Tibetan Buddhism are the Nyingma, or school of the 'earlier translations', originated in the 8th century, with the teaching of Padmasambhava. The Sakya school was established in the 11th century by Drogmi Lotsawa (993-1050). The Gelug school was founded by Je Tsongkhapa (1357-1419) in the 15th century as a reformation of the earlier Kadam school inspired by Atisha's teaching. The Kagyü which originated with Marpa Chökyi Lodrö, the translator, arose in the beginning of the 11th century, inspired by the great Indian saint, Nāropa.

[20] The Kālacakra Tantra is one of the highest Buddhist tantras. In the new schools of Tibetan Buddhism in particular, the Kālacakra is considered to be the most complete tantra. Its teaching comprises outer, inner and alternative levels, roughly corresponding to the outer universe, inner structure of the human body and the purified aspect of the maṇḍala and the deity.

the Islamic invasion that had also conquered and destroyed Oddiyana and Shambhala,[21] the Anuyoga teachings in Trusha disappeared.

In any case, what characterizes the Anuyoga method? Anuyoga uses transformation, just as the higher tantras do in general. However, Anuyoga knowledge of the base is different from that of the higher tantras. Anuyoga knowledge of the base, including the three primordial wisdoms, is the same in every respect as that of Dzogchen. But how does one enter into the state and obtain realization? For that, Anuyoga uses the method of transformation. Dzogchen does not use transformation. The method used in Dzogchen is called self-liberation and in self-liberation there is not even the concept of pure and impure vision. But the general tantric system of transformation is based on the idea of pure and impure vision, and of transforming impure vision into pure vision. However, the Anuyoga system of transformation and the general methods of transformation of the higher tantras are different.

In fact, in all tantric traditions such as Kalachakra, Hevajra, Chakrasamvara, Guhyasamaja,[22] transformation is a gradual process. To effect the transformation one reads a text which describes the various gradual steps of visualization of the deity and the dimension of the mandala.[23] Once one has transformed oneself into the deity, one visualizes the details, including the numbers of arms and legs that one has and the colors and ornaments. In that way, reading the text and doing the visualization one builds up the manifesta-

[21] Oḍḍiyāna and Śambhala are ancient lands that witnessed the origin and spread of Tantrism. In particular, Śambhala and its kings were connected to the Kālacakra Tantra.
[22] Hevajra and Cakrasaṃvara are two of the main 'mother' tantras of the new schools of Tibetan Buddhism, while the Guhyasamāja is a 'father' tantra and possibly one of the earliest tantras. The Guhyasamāja tantra spread in Tibet also during the earlier propagation of Buddhism; thus it is found in both the Nyingma and the new schools.
[23] In Tantra, the maṇḍala is the pure dimension that is the abode of the deity. In the stage of development a tantric practitioner visualizes the maṇḍala as a representation of the universe. However, more generally, a maṇḍala can refer to the dimension of our real nature.

tion of oneself as the deity. This is called the development stage.[24] Having done this, one integrates one's manifestation with one's existence—through prana energy,[25] by visualizing chakras[26] and particularly, by using the sound of mantras. Integration means that, at this stage, one no longer feels that the transformation and one's body are separate. This is called the accomplishing stage.[27] Thus there are two stages, and by developing them gradually, in the end one achieves the union of these two stages called Mahamudra,[28] the original significance of this term. That is why all the Mahasiddhas first did this gradual practice and in the end they discarded everything, showing the signs of being Mahasiddhas.[29] Thus, for this tantric system, gradual development is very important. But in Anuyoga there is the knowledge that from the beginning our condition is perfect in the three primordial wisdoms. Since from the beginning we possess that potentiality, we do not need to create or develop anything. Thus, the crucial point is to discover that state and be in it. That is why transformation in Anuyoga is instantaneous.

We can understand this principle through the symbolic transmission which uses the example of the mirror. The mirror has infinite potentiality and this is similar to the infinite potentiality of the three primordial wisdoms present in us from the beginning. We do not need to create anything anew or to develop anything. We just need the method to discover it provided by the teaching and the transmission. For instance, for the reflections to appear in a mirror the secondary cause of objects must be present in front of the

---

[24] Development stage (Tib. *bskyed rim*): first of the two stages that comprise all the practice of the higher tantras.
[25] Prāṇa (Tib. *rlung, srog rlung*) represents the vital energy of the individual that, according to the functions it performs in the human body, is given different names.
[26] Cakra (Tib. *rtsa 'khor*): energetic centers of the body. The main ones are found along the central axis of the body, from the crown of the head to the sacrum.
[27] Accomplishing stage (Tib. *rdzogs rim*): second of the two stages that comprise all the practices of the higher tantras.
[28] Tib. *phyag rgya chen po*.
[29] Tib. *grub chen*, an adept of Tantrism who has accomplished all siddhis, i.e. who is fully realized.

mirror, otherwise reflections do not appear. When reflections appear, the mirror and the objects interact with each other, and the reflections manifest through the infinite potentiality of the mirror. Color, form, size and the other characteristics of the objects appear instantly in a mirror, not gradually. For that reason we do not need to construct anything gradually.

However, although Anuyoga's explanation of the base is the same as that of Dzogchen, the method through which one obtains realization is different. For that reason Anuyoga belongs to the path of transformation. In Tibet, Anuyoga was originally taught by Guru Padmasambhava. But Padmasambhava only taught a general knowledge of Anuyoga; he did not come to Tibet carrying all the Anuyoga texts with him. For the sake of future generations, he advised the translators to travel to Trusha; that is how we now have the complete Anuyoga teaching in Tibetan.

THE PATH: THE ESSENCE OF THE PRACTICE

The Path refers to the knowledge that arises in us upon the discovery of our real nature. At the moment of discovering one's real nature, certainly there is no difference between oneself and Samantabhadra. But Samantabhadra[30] dwells permanently in that state, while we remain in that state only for two seconds or so and then immediately fall into dualistic vision. Therefore, we need to apply the practice in order to slowly develop our capacity.

At the beginning, we may dwell in our real potentiality or real nature for five or ten seconds in a period of twenty-four hours. Then, applying the practice more and more, we may be able to remain for some minutes, then for some hours, thus becoming Dzogchen yogins.

To be a Dzogchen yogin is to no longer be conditioned. Although one lives a normal life, one dwells in the state of instant presence, one's real nature.

---

[30] Samantabhadra (Tib. *kun tu bzang po*) is the primordial Buddha, a symbol for the primordial state of the individual.

Even if, at the beginning, we have no capacity to remain in a state of instant presence, at least we should not be distracted. Our problem is that we are always distracted. For that reason the advice is given to always be aware, to be present. Being present also enhances our capacity for presence, till at a certain point one can be present continuously twenty-four hours at a time.

Some people think that if they were to maintain presence always, they would not be able to do anything else. This is not true. We can do everything when we are present, even work. Actually, if we are present it is much better because we do our work more precisely. Problems arise when we are distracted. For example, if we are distracted while preparing a meal, when we cut the meat we may also cut a finger.

There are different ways in which we can practice, in a ritual way or in a more simple way, but the crucial point is to be present. When being present we should also relax because if we are not relaxed we charge ourselves up and this leads to an accumulation of tension. Accumulation of tension is the cause of many problems. When we are present we can discover the roots of problems such as attachment and fear. Thus, it is very important that we try to apply the practice with an emphasis on the essence of the practice.

When practice is mentioned, some people immediately conceive it as chanting mantras or praying. These are also aspects of practice. Others have the opposite attitude; they are attracted to the Dzogchen teaching because they think in Dzogchen there is nothing to do and one can be free. It is true in Dzogchen there is no obligation to do anything in particular. One is totally free, but within the frame of being aware and undistracted. If we are distracted we will encounter many problems. Some people, feeling they have a modern outlook, say they are attracted to Dzogchen because the Dzogchen principle is not linked to pujas, or chanting in a religious style, and they dislike chanting and so on. It is important to recognize these attitudes.

If one wants to follow Dzogchen, one must be completely free, un-conditioned by opinions; only then can one discover one's real nature and deal with every situation. It does not matter if a practice involves chanting, a rite or a religious form. It is up to us, if we wish to participate in it or not. It is not indispensable that everything we do in terms of practice be strictly in accord with Buddhist tradition. We can integrate all kinds of traditions if they are necessary and prove to be useful. But integration does not mean taking something from here and something from there, and creating a mixture by putting these different things together.

That amounts to creating confusion, not integration. Integration means that first we have discovered our real nature and dwell in it. Now we are in the center of our total dimension; if we need something we can make use of it, no matter what tradition it belongs to.

Some people pay exaggerated attention to names and titles of teachings. In reality all teachings are relative in the sense that, if at a certain moment of our life we need them, we apply them. If we don't need them we don't apply them. For example, people who are agitated need to coordinate their energy; others who are ill need to overcome their illness; still others who are affected by negative provocations need to get rid of them. In these cases, we must apply certain practices in order to overcome these problems: these are relative practices. When we need them and we have the transmission, we can apply them. We have a nice example to illustrate this point. If you have a raincoat that you like very much for its color or cut, you wear it when it rains. If you were to use this raincoat when it is not raining just because you like it, people would consider you strange. It is not a sensible thing to do. It would mean you do not know how to work with circumstances. Relative practice means that we use it when we need it, and thus it is beneficial for us.

THE IMPORTANCE OF GURUYOGA

The main, most important, practice in Dzogchen is Guruyoga. *Guru* means teacher and *yoga* means knowledge. Our real nature, that we discover upon being introduced by the teacher through the three transmissions, is also the real nature of the teacher himself. There is no difference.

To do Guruyoga means to become more and more familiar with the knowledge of our real nature. Guruyoga is a guideline for the practice. Even when we do relative or secondary practices, we begin them by doing Guruyoga. Guruyoga is indispensable for a practitioner. Any moment one feels the impulse, one should do Guruyoga.

However, one must understand what Guruyoga means in this context. In the paths of Sutra, in Hinayana and Mahayana, there is no mention of Guruyoga. In those systems one applies Refuge and Bodhichitta but Guruyoga is a different method. In Tantra it is the teacher who teaches us the path of transformation. We live an ordinary life, we have dualistic vision and we lack pure vision: therefore we are unable to receive the path of transformation in the ways it is transmitted by the Dharmakaya or by the Sambhogakaya. This is because to see we depend on our two eyes. If we were to encounter a rainbow body we could not see it. We don't have the 'third eye'; we only visualize it as a symbol of wisdom. If we close our eyes we cannot see. If we close our ears we cannot hear. We totally depend on the organs of the senses which are material, so they can perceive only what is material. For example, if there were many beings of the intermediate state[31] in front of us, since we do not have the capacity, we could not see even one of them.

For that reason the teacher, during the initiation, instructs you to visualize the place you are in not as an ordinary dimension but as a Mandala of five-colored light, and your body not as an ordinary body but as that of a deity. We apply these instructions and we do the visualizations; at that moment the teacher empowers us with Mantra and visualization, and in this way we receive the initiation. The content of the initiation then becomes our path and later, any time we apply the practice, we do the same transformation.

---

[31] Tib. *bar do*: here, the intermediate state between death and rebirth.

Thus the source from which we receive this method is the teacher and not the Dharmakaya or the Sambhogakaya. First the teacher transforms himself into the deity, then explains to us how to do the transformation and then empowers us. Therefore, what is most important is not that deity, but the teacher. This is the reason why Guruyoga is common to all traditions of Vajrayana. Since the Vajrayana path employs gradual transformation, in Vajrayana the Guruyoga is presented in that way, with visualizations, invocations and recitation of Mantras.

GURUYOGA IN DZOGCHEN

Although Tantra and Dzogchen use the same term, 'Guruyoga', the sense is different. In Dzogchen there are no limitations; one can do Guruyoga in a Vajrayana style or, in a simpler way, one can recognize the real undifferentiated state of one's teachers and oneself. Then one remains five seconds, or one minute, or ten minutes, whichever is appropriate, in the state, permeated with the knowledge that all one's teachers, all enlightened beings and oneself are not different: this is called Guruyoga.

The state of Guruyoga is the primordial state of Samantabhadra, Vajrasattva, all the lineage masters and all our teachers. When we do Guruyoga in a simple way, it is important to unify all our teachers. We have limited ideas, thinking that since some of our teachers are not Dzogchen practitioners we cannot unify them. That is a limitation. The real nature of all teachers is not different, because the Dharmakaya is not different. We should unify them all. That is meaningful for ourselves. We apply Guruyoga for the sake of our realization, not to support the teacher's status, so we must go beyond limitations.

Our responsibility is to become realized. Eventually, if we gain the capacity to teach others, we can teach. But if we have no realization and go around teaching, this creates problems. Some people have no realization but want to benefit others. Regarding this, there is an appropriate saying in

Tibet, 'Someone with a broken neck cannot help someone with a broken head'. That means it is better to cure oneself, and when one acquires the potentiality to help others, one can help them. But first, one needs to build that potentiality.

On receiving Dzogchen teachings one is asked to do Guruyoga. A person who wishes to do dream practice or night practice should do Guruyoga. A person who wants to prepare for his or her death or wants to gain a certain knowledge of the intermediate state should do Guruyoga, rather than the Phowa or transference of consciousness.[32] Guruyoga is much more important than any type of transference of consciousness.

So the foremost practice is Guruyoga. This does not mean that one should do only Guruyoga and nothing else. If we have the time and the wish, we can do any kind of practice, but the only one required is Guruyoga. That, simply stated, is the path to be followed.

THE CONDUCT OF A PRACTITIONER

The path consists of the point of view, meditation and conduct.[33] The point of view is the knowledge of the Base; meditation refers to the understanding and application of methods; conduct is our behavior.

Behavior is a very important factor for practitioners. Even if we have learned fantastic methods, we do not always apply that practice or remain in that state. For example, if we participate in a collective practice that takes half hour or an hour, we may feel very good. After that, the practice ends and we go home to watch television, to work or attend some engagement; we are no longer doing the practice. So in the twenty-four hours of the day our practice consists only of one or two hours. For the other twenty-two hours we are always distracted and, following our emotions, do many useless

---

[32] Transference of consciousness (Tib. *'pho ba*): a method to transfer one's consciousness to a pure realm or to a pure dimension at the time of death.
[33] Tib. *lta ba, sgom pa, spyod pa.*

things, creating tensions and problems. Thus, our spiritual activities take only a small portion of our day.

If we follow Dzogchen we must try to make all the twenty-four hours of the day become practice, and not concentrate simply on one or two hours. To practice for one or two hours is excellent but it is not sufficient to gain realization.

BEING PRESENT

How does one do twenty-four hours of continuous practice? A very simple way is to be aware and not to be distracted. Some people find this very difficult, while others consider that simply not being distracted is not in itself a spiritual practice; they conceive of spiritual practice as the recitation of mantras and similar things. However, to be aware and undistracted is much more meaningful than reciting mantras while distracted. Sometimes, if one recites mantras, maybe one accumulates some merit, but practice is very much related to the intention of the mind. Some people recite the mantra of Avalokiteshvara with their voice, but with their mind they are thinking about their business. This can never become an important practice. Even if one does not recite a single mantra but tries to be aware and undistracted, one immediately recognizes one's own bad intentions.

Bad intentions bring bad actions and the accumulation of negative karma. By being present one can stop this process. This is also the very essence of the Mahayana practice. In Mahayana one works with intentions; when there is a bad intention one changes it and cultivates a good intention. One can do that if one is not distracted. If one is charged up or tense for example, with awareness one immediately becomes aware of that and relaxes. Thus, if one is present one can discover all the mind patterns. It may be a little difficult; in fact, some people who have followed the Dzogchen teaching for a short time complain that they are often distracted, but all our life has been a distraction.

It is not easy to always be aware and undistracted. Although we know that this is difficult, we can learn to be so if we wish; there is a method for learning. For example, on Sunday when you have free time and are alone, you can try to do the practice of being aware. You observe whether you are present or distracted. When you observe in this way, you discover right away what your condition is.

You may suddenly have the idea of writing a letter. When this happens, if you may become distracted by that thought and start writing immediately. That means you are distracted. Being aware means that you know you are thinking of writing a letter. You decide to write. You prepare a paper and pen and you start to write the letter, while being aware that you are writing. When you are thinking about what to write you are aware that you are thinking that. You maintain full awareness during the time you are writing till the end. When you have finished writing you fold the letter, and you place it in an envelope. You are aware that you have finished writing and are placing the letter in the envelope, and that now you are writing the address. Now you must put the letter in the post box. You take the letter and you walk, knowing you are walking, to post the letter.

On the way you may meet someone you know. He greets you and asks where you are going. At that time, you do not become distracted, but know, 'I have met this person, he is asking me where I am going and I want to reply. Now I am replying, we are talking, now I am continuing my walk to post the letter.' You can do this for an hour. At the beginning it is a bit difficult to be aware, but the next day it will be easier and in the end one will not need any effort. I do not say one can accomplish this practice in just a few weeks but one can learn in the way I explained. This is a very important practice.

ORDINARY PRESENCE AND
INSTANT PRESENCE

The knowledge of our real nature is called instant presence. or being in the state of *rigpa*. That is the main point of our practice, but we cannot always be in that state. Nonetheless, if we have ordinary presence we can integrate instant presence into that very easily. What is the difference between instant presence and ordinary presence? Ordinary presence implies a twofold effort: the effort to continue to be present and the effort to be without distraction. If you are in the state of instant presence, you don't need any kind of effort. If you apply effort, it means you are no longer in a state of instant presence. When we are capable of remaining totally in the state of instant presence for hours and hours we are really Dzogchen yogins.

ULTIMATE PURIFICATION

With the power of contemplation, all our negative karma can be purified. In general, when we feel the need to do purification in an ordinary way, we may think of the famous purification method of Vajrasattva.[34] Yet, a still more powerful purification is to dwell in our real nature; that is the supreme purification. Those who lack such understanding think that, since they have accumulated much negative karma, it would be better to apply a common method of purification instead of Guruyoga. Indeed, to obtain total realization one needs a complete purification, but the most powerful method of purification is to be in the state of the real nature.

In a Sutra,[35] the Buddha gave the following important example. A person who dedicates his or her whole life to purifying himself, making offerings

[34] Vajrasattva (Tib. *rDo rje sems dpa'*) is the Buddha who symbolizes the principle of the union of the five 'Buddha families' i.e. the five main psychological types according to which Tantric practitioners are traditionally classified: Vajra, Padma, Ratna, Karma and Buddha. Its practice is common to all of the four schools of Tibetan Buddhism and used mainly to purify obscurations.
[35] The *Samādhirājasūtra*, or *Sūtra of the King of Samādhi*, a fundamental sūtra in the Vijñānavāda school of Mahāyāna Buddhism.

to the Buddhas, visiting temples, and maintaining vows, accumulates much merit. Yet, in terms of obtaining total realization, compared to that merit, if a person remains in the state of contemplation—in his or her real nature—for the short time it takes for an ant to go from the nose to the forehead, that is much more beneficial. Through this example we can understand how remaining even a short time in a state of contemplation can purify us and increase our clarity.

Some practitioners do a personal retreat for a week or so, trying to be in a state of Guruyoga but at the end they complain that they are still the same, and that neither clarity nor realization has arisen; they are surprised. This is not surprising. We have lived countless lives and in these lives we have accumulated infinite karma so it is not easy to purify ourselves or increase our clarity. However, if we apply the practice and we dwell more and more precisely in our real nature we can certainly develop greater clarity and all other qualities.

THE AWARENESS OF CIRCUMSTANCES

The principle in Dzogchen is to be aware. In the Sutra you receive a vow, you have a rule prescribing what you can and cannot do, and you follow that rule just as it is set out. But in Dzogchen there is no such rule. Why? It is because all rules are connected to relative circumstances. For example, what was considered positive many centuries ago may be viewed as negative in our day. What is considered good in the East may be seen as bad in the West. No rule exists that is appropriate in every respect for the various times, places and circumstances. So what we really need to learn is to be aware. We do not follow rules and we become autonomous. Thus, we do not depend on anything.

If we think that as practitioners of Dzogchen we do not need to have respect for anything, for any rule, we are not good Dzogchen practitioners.

In Dzogchen, one must be aware. With awareness one must know how to work with the circumstances. In the circumstances there are rules; a country may have established rules and if one travels in or lives in that country, one must respect such rules. If one does not respect those rules one can suffer negative consequences.

To be aware of the circumstances is the correct approach. Some people consider that this is not Dzogchen and do not care, but we need to have respect for all sentient beings and for all their dimensions. Although in Dzogchen there are no rules, we do re-educate ourselves to be aware. Our responsibility does not lie in a rule but in ourselves. To apply this principle is not an easy task, but it is not impossible. We can learn and develop whatever we intend to. At the beginning all is difficult but once learned there is no problem.

For example, most people know how to drive. At the start it is not easy to learn to drive, but once one has learned one can drive anywhere with no problems. Why is that? Because we exercise presence during driving, and we do that even while talking to someone, or looking to the side: we are not distracted and always aware. If we lose that presence we can have accidents. However, our life is not just driving; our life is eating, cooking, working in an office, and particularly meeting people and discussing things with them. If we learn that, we can be aware in all these activities, without necessarily being distracted.

DIRECT INTRODUCTION
TO OUR REAL NATURE

Garab Dorje, the first and most important master of Dzogchen in our ep-och, made three statements which represent the summary of his teachings. These three statements contain all the principles of the manner in which we learn Dzogchen, the manner of teaching it, and the manner of applying the Dzogchen methods.

The first statement is, 'direct introduction'. We understand that there are three transmissions—oral, symbolic and direct; the first two are a sort of preparation for direct introduction. Someone who has good karma—that is, he was a Dzogchen practitioner in his past life even though in his present life as a human being he is not yet engaging in Dzogchen practice,—when he is introduced by the teacher through the oral transmission or the symbolic transmission, he can awaken.

That happens because of the preparation from a past life, but this is not the case for everyone. In most cases, the three transmissions are given one after the other, and in that way one also can comprehend that the direct transmission is the most important one. Direct introduction deals with the three experiences of emptiness, clarity and sensation of pleasure. These three experiences correspond to the Mind, Voice and Body, respectively.

The teacher explains to us how to produce these experiences, and then, on the basis of these experiences, we work with the teacher to discover our state. In fact, our real nature is beyond explanations, it cannot be shown nor taught. In the Sutras the Buddha said that the Prajñaparamita or Transcendent Wisdom is beyond explanation. Even if a teacher explains over many days the meaning of the Prajñaparamita, in a real sense he cannot explain it. The tantras also state that we cannot explain our real nature. It seems there is nothing to be done. You may remember that in the movie *The Little Buddha* there is a scene where a monk chants the words of a Mahayana Sutra, the Prajñaparamita.[36] This Sutra is given great importance, and considered the heart of all Mahayana teachings. For that reason, in all the Mahayana traditions of Tibet, Japan and China, there exists the custom of chanting this Sutra. The Sutra starts by saying that there is no nose, no tongue, no ears, and then goes on to say that there is nothing. In conclusion the Sutra says that there is no path, there is no wisdom, there is no obtainment and also no

---

[36] Skt.: *Prajñāpāramitāhṛdayasūtra.*

non-obtainment. This means that everything is a concept and that to discover the real meaning of Prajñaparamita one should go beyond all concepts.

How does one transcend all concepts? Not by talking or intellectual reasoning. One can transcend concepts only through experience, and through that come to discovery. This is something that it is essential to understand.

THIRTY WORDS *of* ADVICE *from the* HEART

LONGCHENPA'S TEXT

I bow at the feet of my Guru, the protector, the supreme of the
triple gem,
Who from the great clouds of aspirations, the wisdom
encompassing the space expanse of reality,
Makes the stream of nectar of warm rays of compassion fall
Ripening the buds of the three enlightened dimensions in the
fields of the students.

By the power of my aspirations I was able to become a disciple
in the supreme lineage of accomplishment;
Yet I have spent my time uselessly, avoiding effort, and now this
life is coming to its twilight.
My intention was to behave like an ascetic, but now I am a
distressed man and, seeing others like me,
I have spoken these thirty words of advice to exhort my mind
in the spirit of renunciation.

I | Alas! Having gathered, by various means, a large circle of people
around yourself,
You may possess a prosperous monastic estate;
Yet, this is only the cause of quarrels and attachment for one's
mind.
Live in solitude! This is my advice from the heart.

II | You may display to the crowd expertise in village rites
In preventing children's deaths and subduing evil spirits;
Yet, because of craving for food and wealth, your mind is
carried off by demons.
Subdue your mind! This is my advice from the heart.

III | Having collected large tributes from poor people
You may build big shrines, make donations, and so forth;
Yet, this only causes you to accumulate evil deeds on virtuous
grounds.
Make your mind virtuous! This is my advice from the heart.

IV | You may teach the Dharma to others out of desire for
greatness,
And with gross deceitful ways, surround yourself with a circle
of important and humble people;
Yet a mind that grasps things as real is a cause of pride.
Have only short term plans! This is my advice from the heart.

V | Commerce, loaning with interest, cheating, and so forth, are
wrong means of securing one's livelihood.
You can make large donations with the wealth amassed in these
ways;

Yet merits resting on the desire for fame are the source of the
  eight worldly concerns.
Be averse to such activities! This is my advice from the heart.

VI | Acting as a peacemaker, witness, or involving yourself in
  lawsuits, you may settle others' disputes,
And think that you are working for the benefit of beings;
Yet doing such things is a cause for ambition to arise.
Be free from hope and fear! This is my advice from the heart.

VII | You may have subjects, wealth, retinue, merits and your fame
May fill the entire world;
Yet at the time of death these things will be of no benefit
  whatsoever.
Be diligent in spiritual practice! This is my advice from the
  heart.

VIII | Stewards, close friends, principals, and cooks
Are indeed the pillar of life of the monastic community;
Yet commitment to these roles is a cause for worry.
Diminish busy involvements! This is my advice from the heart.

IX | Carrying religious images, statues, offerings, scriptures, a stove
And all your requirements, you may go to a mountain
  hermitage;
Yet the paraphernalia meant to satisfy immediate needs are the
  source of quarrels and problems.
Have no needs! This is my advice from the heart.

X | In these times of degeneration, you may scold
The unruly people around you, thinking it will benefit them;
Yet, doing this causes negative emotions.
Speak calmly! This is my advice from the heart.

XI | Without any selfish motive, you may tell people you love,
With the intention of helping them, their mistakes;
Yet although what you say is true, (your words) are like a tumor
in their heart.
Speak gently! This is my advice from the heart.

XII | With the thought of preserving the purity of the Teaching
You may engage in discussions, defending your opinion and
refuting that of others;
Yet in this way you create disturbing thoughts.
Remain silent! This is my advice from the heart.

XIII | You may honor in a sectarian way
Your master, your lineage of teaching and your philosophical
school;
Yet to praise oneself and despise others is a cause for
attachment and anger.
Give this (attitude) up! This is my advice from the heart.

XIV | Having heard and analyzed different kinds of Teachings,
You may think that comprehending the faults of others is
wisdom;
Yet this is (precisely) the cause for accumulating evil deeds for
yourself.
Maintain pure vision! This is my advice from the heart.

XV | Proffering mindless talk on emptiness and disregarding cause
and effect,
You may think that non-action is the ultimate point of the
Teaching;
Yet to abandon the two accumulations will destroy the good
fortune of spiritual practice.
Integrate them both! This is my advice from the heart.

XVI | You may think that the path of another's body
That involves the descent of semen, related to the meaning of
the third (initiation) will enhance your practice;
Yet through this material path many excellent yogins have been
deceived.
Rely on the path of liberation! This is my advice from the heart.

XVII | To give initiations to unqualified people
And distribute sacred substances to the crowd
Is the cause of slander and breach of commitments.
Be serious! This is my advice from the heart.

XVIII | You may think that wandering naked in public and
Other peculiar behavior is the deliberate conduct (of a yogin);
Yet this is the cause for worldly people to lose faith (in the
Teaching).
Be considerate! This is my advice from the heart.

XIX | With the desire to be the highest one in the place where you
live,
You may develop a good attitude and become very learned;
Yet this is the cause for falling from an elevated status to the
lowest position.
Be neither tight nor loose! This is my advice from the heart.

XX | Wherever you stay, in a city, monastery or mountain hermitage,
Do not seek close friends,
Befriend all with neither intimacy nor hostility.
Keep your independence! This is my advice from the heart.

XXI | Behaving like a hypocrite, you may honor impressively the
faithful patrons
Who provide you with sustenance;
Yet to feign in order to (please) others is to bind oneself.
Apply the conduct of experiencing all equally as one taste! This
is my advice from the heart.

XXII | The methods based on interdependence (found in) countless
books about such matters as divination, astrology, medicine
Are cause for omniscient knowledge;
Yet becoming attached to various subjects will disrupt one's
contemplation.
Reduce the subjects you study! This is my advice from the heart.

XXIII | When you live in a house, leave aside furnishing the house.
In the midst of solitude you may arrange to have all comforts;
Yet, this only consumes one's life in triviality.
Put off all these activities! This is my advice from the heart.

XXIV | You may persevere in spiritual practice—learning and virtue—
And thus some of your qualities may become remarkable;
Yet whatever you cling to will bind your mind.
Learn how to be free and without limitations! This is my advice
from the heart.

XXV | You may think that subduing those who are to be confronted,
with various (rites) of black magic and protection,
Such as causing hail and thunderbolts (to fall), is enlightened
activity;
Yet to burn the mind of another being will cause you to be
reborn in lower realms.
Keep a low profile! This is my advice from the heart.

XXVI | You may have collected many useful profound texts—
philosophical scriptures,
Spoken advice, transcribed teachings,
Yet if you do not practice, at the time of death, books don't
help.
Observe your mind! This is my advice from the heart.

XXVII | When you practice wholeheartedly, you may have meditative
experiences, discuss them with others,
Write commentaries, and sing songs of realization.
Although these are manifestations (of the practice), they will
(only) increase thoughts.
Remain in the state beyond concepts! This is my advice from
the heart.

XXVIII | When thoughts arise, it is crucial that you look at them
directly,
And when you have clearly seen mind's (nature), it is essential to
abide in it.
Although there is nothing to meditate upon, it is important to
remain in meditation.
Maintain the undistracted state! This is my advice from the
heart.

XXIX| Within (the knowledge of) emptiness, act (in accordance) with
the law of cause and effect,
And when you have understood (the principle of) non-action,
Keep the three commitments and strive to benefit all beings
with non-conceptual compassion.
Unite the two accumulations! This is my advice from the heart.

XXX | I have followed many learned and realized masters and received
many profound instructions,
I have seen a few profound Sutras and Tantras and also
examined them a little;
Yet whilst knowing them, I do not apply them.
Alas! I'm just deceiving myself!

For myself and those like me, I have spoken these thirty words
of advice from the heart.

Through the merit of this composition written with the desire
to attain liberation,
May all beings be liberated from the wilderness of conditioned
existence, and be guided to the state of great bliss.
May I become a supreme son who walks in the footsteps of the
Buddhas of the three times, of their heirs and of the great
ascetics.

Thus impelled by a slight sense of the arising of renunciation,
I, Tsultrim Lodrö,[37] composed these Thirty Words of
Advice from the Heart.

---

[37] The name Longchenpa received when he was ordained as a novice monk at Samye
monastery.

COMMENTARY *by*
CHÖGYAL NAMKHAI NORBU

L ONGCHENPA WAS A GREAT Dzogchen practitioner. On the basis of his experience he wrote thirty words of advice for his students. These thirty advices concern certain situations of which it is important to be aware. Maybe not all of them are relevant to our situation, but undoubtedly many of these can be useful for our life. We should remember those which are more meaningful to us, and integrate them in our daily life.

The title of Longchenpa's text is *Nyingtam Sumchupa*.[38] *Nyingtam* means heartfelt words or words from the heart; that is, words that one does not just say to anyone, but only to those close, as advice. *Sumchupa* means thirty verses. Longchenpa presents this advice as if directed to himself and, by implication, also to his students. The advice concerns mainly persons like Longchenpa; he was a monk and a teacher, so his advice is appropriate for that condition. However the text also contains much advice that can be useful for everybody.

HOMAGE TO THE MASTER

I bow at the feet of my guru, the protector, the supreme of the triple gem,

Who from the great clouds of aspirations, the wisdom encompassing the space expanse of reality,

---

[38] *sNying gtam sum cu pa.*

Makes the stream of nectar of the warm rays of compassion fall
Ripening the buds of the three enlightened dimensions in the fields of
    the students.

With this verse, Longchenpa pays homage to the teacher. He compares his teacher to space and in this space, clouds form the teachings which, like rain descending upon the earth, mature the disciples' minds.

THE EXHORTATION

By the power of my aspirations I became a disciple of the supreme
    masters of the lineage of accomplishment;
Yet, having spent my time uselessly, I have not made any effort, and
    now this life is coming to its twilight.
My intention was to behave like an ascetic, but now I am a distressed
    man and seeing others like me,
I have spoken these thirty words of advice to exhort my mind in the
    spirit of renunciation.

Longchenpa says that because of his fortunate karma in this life he entered the path, met excellent teachers and was taught by them. Despite this good opportunity he passed his time distractedly, and his life was like the growing shadows of mountains that foretell evening. This is true for us as well: while time passes we are always distracted by useless activities.

Longchenpa had the good intention to engage in spiritual practice and other good deeds during his life but, because of his attitude and what he really had been doing, that intention became a mere wish. When he saw that his intentions did not match his actions, he felt sad. For that reason he wrote these words of advice to himself and others like him.

Unlike us, as a young man Longchenpa studied the Dharma under many teachers and later spent most of his life in the mountains. Thus, it seems that Longchenpa wrote this text of advice when he was still young, before deciding to set off for the mountains to dedicate himself to practice.

THE FIRST WORD OF ADVICE

Alas! Having gathered, by various means, a large circle of people around yourself,

You may possess a prosperous monastic estate;

Yet, this is only the cause of quarrels and attachment for one's mind.

Live in solitude! This is my advice from the heart.

Through various means we gather many people around ourselves; for example, in a monastery we gather many monks, and as teachers we increase the number of our students. Once this is accomplished, we may think that now all the good conditions are present, but in reality all this is a source of quarrels and of attachment. Thus it is better we stay alone and free. I often think this: I have many students who ask me to come here and there, and I try to make them happy, but my students don't always follow my advice to apply themselves to the practice. Sometimes they fight with each other, creating many problems, and I also bear the consequences of that. I tell them that we have commitments to maintain. I maintain the commitments with my students, but this is not sufficient. Between students too there must be mutual respect; if they do not respect each other problems arise. We, teacher and students, are in the same boat, so to speak, traveling to a very far destination. If one creates a problem in a boat it affects everyone else in that boat. This is just an example, but Longchenpa gave this advice for such situations.

THE SECOND WORD OF ADVICE

You may display to the crowd expertise in village rites

In preventing children's deaths and subduing evil spirits;

Yet, because of craving for food and wealth, your mind is carried off by demons.

Subdue your mind! This is my advice from the heart.

If you are a monk or a Lama people invite you to perform rites, or pujas[39] as they are commonly known. Many monks and Lamas involved in that become puja-monks or puja-lamas. When I first arrived in Sikkim, India, where I was intending to live, I had no one to sponsor me, and I had to make money to live. Although I wanted to work I was unable get a job. At that time, many people, hearing that I was an incarnation, a learned Lama, asked me to perform rites in their homes. So I started to perform various rites for them at their houses. At the end of the rites, these households would offer me money and food. In that way, doing one or two pujas a week, I could make my livelihood. The families for whom I was performing rites advised other families, who also needed a Lama to do a puja at their house, to invite me. So my schedule became busier, as now I was performing rites three times a week; and after some weeks, I had to perform them every day; in that way I was becoming a puja-lama. I had no problem earning a living, but rites performed in this way are just for one's livelihood. Many monks and Lamas in monasteries support themselves that way, by performing village rites.[40] Longchenpa refers to that.

'Preventing children's deaths'[41] refers to rites for curing children when they are ill or suffer from another problem. Usually, people invite monks or Lamas to perform such rites. In Tibet, people in the countryside are used to inviting monks and Lamas to perform rites when cattle, horses, and other domestic animals are struck down by a disease, or to perform rites in order to eliminate the negativity responsible for bad luck and misfortunes in the family. 'Subduing evil spirits'[42] refers to rites for eliminating provocations. Where there is some provocation, usually people in Tibet ask an expert for a divination and if the divination indicates that specific rites need to be done

---

[39] Pūja is a Sanskrit term which is commonly used to indicate the performance of a rite.
[40] Tib. *grong chog.*
[41] Tib. *sri'u gso.*
[42] Tib. *'dre 'dul.*

in order to overcome the provocation, since common people do not know how to perform rites, it is the custom to invite a Lama. For example, if astrological calculations show that a person's life condition is negatively affected in the current year, customarily people think of requesting a monastery to perform some rites.

One cannot ask a monastery to perform rites for oneself without making an offering. Thus, one offers money and other necessities, and the monastery performs the rites or dispatches monks to perfom these rites in one's house. If a monk or other practitioners have the qualifications for performing such rites, they become puja-lamas. Such a 'job' creates attachment to money, wealth and food, and that is why some monks and Lamas agree to perform pujas in the first place. In this case, one's mind is dominated by the demons, in that one is not applying the practice for the right purpose.

While I lived in Sikkim I acted as a puja-lama for many months. After some time, I received news that my father and my brother were held in prison in Tibet. The Chinese were accusing them because I was reported to be in India, working against the Chinese. Although other Tibetans were indeed involved in anti-Chinese activities, I never participated in these. Thus I decided to return to Tibet in order to prove that I was not working against the Chinese.

I traveled to the border between Sikkim and Tibet where I stayed for about a week. There, a householder asked me to stay in his house and perform rites for my own sake and theirs while waiting at least a week so as to check out how the situation in Tibet was evolving. I did the puja of Tara for more than a week and during that time, every day I received news that the situation in Tibet was becoming worse and worse. I also had a clear dream which indicated I should not go back to Tibet. The householder advised me not to return to Tibet, because if I were to do so the Chinese, instead of liberating my father and my brother, would put me in prison too. I decided not to set off for Tibet and went back down to Gangtok. However, I did not want to live any longer as a puja-lama. I asked the government of Sikkim for a job; my request was accepted and I was offered one. Everyday I used to work in an office like an ordinary person till I went to Italy. This gave me the opportunity to pursue my studies and to practice.

Considering such situations, Longchenpa reminds us that what is most important is to re-educate our mind, to watch what kind of intention we have, what plans we have. If we see that we have a negative intention, we should change it and cultivate a good intention. We usually take various vows to control our body, speech and mind so as not to create negative karma. If we check our intention with awareness, we can control ourselves with no need of any vow.

THE THIRD WORD OF ADVICE

Having collected large tributes from poor people
You may build big shrines, make donations, and so forth;
Yet, this only causes you to accumulate evil deeds on virtuous
grounds.
Make your mind virtuous! This is my advice from the heart.

There are many people who live in poverty with neither money nor a job. When you are in a position of power you may ask such poor people to pay various tributes, like the taxes or payments that governments and rich land-owners always demand. Through various means, you may travel in different regions asking for money on the pretext that you are raising a large sum of money to build a Stupa, or a big statue of Buddha, or a monastery. Naturally devotees, even if poor, try to come up with something to offer. Or, you may pretend to raise money for charity in order to alleviate the poverty of others. Even if you consider this a virtuous action, in reality it yields the opposite result: many don't have sufficient money for themselves, and thus to take money from them is negative.

Longchenpa's advice here is that instead of doing that, one should re-educate oneself and be virtuous in one's mind and actions. When you are in a position to help others with good intention, even if on a small scale, you should do it. There is no need to make a show of helping others and then direct the funds to other causes.

THE FOURTH WORD OF ADVICE

You may teach the Dharma to others out of desire for greatness,

And with gross deceitful ways, surround yourself with a circle of important and humble people;

Yet a mind that grasps things as real is a cause of pride.

Have only short term plans! This is my advice from the heart.

Desiring to become famous or important, a great teacher for example, you may claim to be a reincarnation, very learned, all-knowing. Even if you do not quite say that, with the same intention you may act in a way meant to show you are a special, spiritual person; with all kinds of means you may control others in order to become a leader. That's how everyone behaves in our society.

For example, at election time, the heads of various political parties beg for votes from electors on the promise of doing many good things. The public becomes convinced by their speeches, and votes for them, but once a candidate wins the election and comes to power, he does everything contrary to what he had promised. That is just an example, but in small groups too we try to do the same. Even if we succeed in our intention, this is just a cause, or the root, for increasing pride and, on the basis of pride, one accumulates many negative actions.

Longchenpa's advice here is to have short term plans. Short term plans mean not concentrating excessively on our future goals. Naturally, some plans are indispensable and need to be made, but we should not always be thinking about plans.

For example if a couple, husband and wife, have this attitude, they will pay respect and help each other for their whole life. If they don't have that attitude, at the first small difficulty, they might think, 'He or she insists on this and that. How can we live all our lives together?'

At the beginning, when they fell in love, their situation was different; everything was lovely. Even if one was mistreated by the other, it still seemed nice. But after three, five, six or ten years everything becomes more difficult. This is because, initially, our emotions make us blind, and we don't see the problems, but with the passing of time, various problems emerge.

At that point we say that we cannot live the rest of our life that way, and that we must divorce. This is the contrary of having short term plans. To have short term plans means to be aware that we are uncertain as to whether we will still be alive tomorrow or not. This is true not only for older people but for the young as well. This is our real condition.

Moreover, for our spiritual practice, making only short term plans is essential. Sometimes we like a certain teaching or spiritual practice, so we write it down with the intention that one day we will apply it. The next day, instead of doing that practice, we meet another teacher and hear of another practice.

Now we like that and think that one day we will apply it. But one day we will come to the last day of our life. At that time, because we did not make any short term plans, we just have a nice collection of teachings and practices. For this reason, here Longchenpa advises us it is better to make only short term plans.

THE FIFTH WORD OF ADVICE

*Commerce, loaning with interest, cheating, and so forth, are wrong
means of securing one's livelihood.*

You can make large donations with the wealth amassed in these ways;

*Yet merits resting on the desire for fame are the source of the eight
worldly concerns.*[43]

Be averse to such activities! This is my advice from the heart.

When we do business, or lend money with interest, we may earn a considerable amount of money and become rich, but, even if later we use this money
to make donations, this is accumulating wealth with improper means. Such
activities are always the cause of worldly concerns, that is, thoughts of becoming famous or powerful. Longchenpa's advice here is that it is better to
feel repugnance for these activities.

If we are spiritual practitioners we feel contempt for samsaric situations; we are not seriously or deeply interested in them. This does not mean
that we feel disgust for or reject everything. In our life, all is relative. In our
life, not everything is how it should be, nonetheless we continue to live.
We accept and integrate the various circumstances of life. This is part of
our awareness. To accept everything with awareness is different from being
completely attached. Some people have an exaggerated liking for this or that:
this is attachment.

However, it does not mean that if you are a good practitioner you cannot
have likings. You can like and enjoy with awareness. In the samsaric condition,
we possess five or six senses, and with the senses we enjoy contact with objects.
When we see an object, a flower for example, we may like it. We observe
its beauty and smell its fragrance. We enjoy looking and smelling. To enjoy
with awareness means to know the real nature of the object and not become

---

[43] Eight worldly concerns (Tib. *'jig rten chos brgyad*): fame and obscurity, pleasure and
pain, gain and loss, praise and blame.

attached to it. In this way, we enjoy without having negative consequences. If we are not aware, we become distracted with our liking for the flower; we want to possess the flower and attempt to have it. Thus, attachment increases, releasing all other emotions, with the ensuing negative karma.

In brief, if one is aware and undistracted the enjoyment of the senses does not pose any problem. If one is distracted, enjoyment always bears negative consequences, even if things appear joyful and gratifying. For that reason, the teaching says that all is illusion. When we see a nice object and we become attached, we resemble a moth which, attracted by a flame at night, flies into it, burns, and dies.

Sometimes we like music very much, but if one is attached to music that is negative, like forest deer who become attracted and distracted by pleasant music played by hunters, who then, allowed to draw closer, kill them. There are many examples of the negative consequences of attachment, related to each of the five senses.

To a Dzogchen practitioner, the enjoyment of the senses is not prohibited, nor must it be renounced. A Dzogchen practitioner may always enjoy sense objects but only on the condition of maintaining presence and avoiding distractions. This is very important.

THE SIXTH WORD OF ADVICE

Acting as a peacemaker, witness, or involving yourself in lawsuits,
   you may settle others' disputes,
And think that you are working for the benefit of beings;
Yet to do such things is a cause for ambition to arise.
Be free from hope and fear! This is my advice from the heart.

To act as a peacemaker trying to make others reach an agreement, for example in a court case, is considered a good action. To act as a witness when you have seen or you know how a problem arose, stating where the truth lies, is also considered positive. Moreover, sometimes you participate in lawsuits, for example, if a group of extraneous people causes a problem to a monastery, you may get involved in the dispute with the intention of helping that monastery, thinking this is a good thing to do.

Even if you think that these actions are positive, they do not yield the benefit one may expect. Often when you want to help it means you have a vested interest in helping. Whenever we do something, we develop tension and fall into either hope or fear.

Longchenpa's advice here is that instead of assuming such responsibilities, we must try to be more in our real nature, not conditioned by hope and fear, as in the Chöd practice when we say, 'I cultivate Bodhichitta beyond hope and fear'.

THE SEVENTH WORD OF ADVICE

You may have subjects, wealth, retinue, merits and your fame
May fill the entire world;
Yet at the time of death these things will be of no benefit whatsoever.
Be diligent in spiritual practice! This is my advice from the heart.

When we become a famous or important person we may have subjects, wealth and money, and many people who support us. Our dimension—a retinue of people who depend on us and fortune which is the result of our own merit—manifests visibly. We want to increase this position even more; our fame is spreading everywhere and still we want to increase it. But even if the entire world is filled with our fame, when our life comes to an end, none of these conditions can help: we move on alone. We cannot take with us even those provisions that one usually takes on a journey. For that reason, dedication to spiritual practice is very important. Spiritual practice will really benefit us when we come to our last day; in particular, the Guruyoga.

To be in the state of Guruyoga is to be in the timeless state of instant presence. When we die, the intermediate state (*bardo*) of the moment of death is very different from the intermediate state of the period between birth and death. At the moment of death, all the functions of the elements of our body dissolve inwardly, one after the other. All the functions of the senses, too, dissolve. The internal dissolution of each of these factors is accompanied by strong experiences. These experiences produce the very intense suffering of the moment of death. But all these dissolutions and experiences occur in time.

As soon as you recognize that you are dying, you should enter the state of Guruyoga. In that way you are beyond time. You notice what is occurring in your body at that moment, such as the dissolution of the elements, but since you are in the state of instant presence, you do not experience suffering in the ordinary way. In that state, death also poses no problem to you. We should dedicate ourselves to the practice of Guruyoga and become good practitioners of that.

It is important to do the practice of Guruyoga also at night. We do not require a complicated dream practice. In the dream, the mind awakens and all the sense consciousnesses are associated with the mind, they are no longer dependent on the sense organs; this dimension is called the mental body. In this dimension one can have many kinds of dreams. Sometimes karmic dreams result from one's previous actions. At times, dreams related to a heavy karma from a past life can also manifest. However, such dreams are rare and do not often occur. For example if you have a dream of an experience you never had in this life, such as a great tragedy, and this dream occurs repeatedly, that indicates it is a karmic dream.

Other karmic dreams can manifest as a result of an event that shocked you when you were a child. For example in 1957, when I was in my country, everyone revolted against the Chinese government. The fight went on for about two months and everyday we were afraid that Chinese soldiers would arrive. At night we were afraid to sleep in our houses or tents, so we would go to sleep in the mountains. It was winter and it was a very hard life. Later, my family and I succeeded in leaving for central Tibet. However our animals were very weak, as it was the spring season. When we arrived in another region we had to stop there for several weeks. On our three month journey, till we reached Lhasa, we were constantly afraid of meeting Chinese soldiers. This affected me considerably. Even today, I sometimes have karmic dreams of Chinese soldiers, although I have no problems with them now. I have visited China many times and while I was there, Chinese soldiers invited me several times to eat with them. But I still feel afraid when I have such dreams. This is an example of a karmic dream. Each one of us can have various dreams of this kind. We have these dreams when we sleep very deeply. When we fall asleep, in these cases, we sleep heavily because we are tired from our daily activities. Even if our sleep is deep, karmic dreams do manifest.

In the early morning around four or five o'clock, we sleep very lightly and at this time we can have dreams of clarity. If there is a continuation of presence, interesting dreams of clarity can easily manifest. If one has an interesting or terrible dream, one can immediately recognize and become aware that one is dreaming. For practitioners, that is crucial. During the daytime we can dedicate only a short time to the practice, trying to be aware. Even if we have learned many fantastic methods we don't always have either the time or the opportunity to apply them, but if one is aware while dreaming one can do these practices within the dream.

In a dream there is seven times more clarity than in the daytime. This is because in the day our senses are dependent on the sense organs, and the sense organs are related to the material world. The mental body of the dream, instead, has no such limitation. Thus, clarity is more intense and so in dreams one can apply various practices and progress in them. Moreover, the dream practice will influence and to a great extent benefit the day practice.

Buddha Shakyamuni said that our life is just like a long dream. We can understand this intellectually but in practice it is difficult to feel that life is like a dream. However, as a result of the practice that one does in dreams, one does not need much effort to believe that life is like a dream. One really has that feeling, and when you really feel that, you do not have a strong attachment. It is not just a matter of becoming indifferent, because we cannot live with indifference. But with our awareness we work with the circumstances, and when we govern our life with awareness, circumstances are not a problem.

THE EIGHTH WORD OF ADVICE

Stewards, close friends, principals, and cooks
Are indeed the pillar of life[44] of the monastic community;
Yet commitment to these roles is a cause for worry.
Diminish busy involvements! This is my advice from the heart.

Monasteries or important people, such as high Lamas, retain stewards (Lamas actually have two kinds of stewards) who administer their property, possessions and wealth. These stewards supervise, for example, the expenditures for food and other necessities. Then we have close friends or close relations, as well as principal relations, that is, important persons or important teachers with whom we need to maintain a good relationship. Finally, there are the cooks, who, in their own way, play a crucial role in monasteries. These people and their roles seem to be indispensable but in reality they are the root of many problems. Just as Patrul Rinpoche[45] said, if you have a goat, you have the problem of the goat; if you have a package of tea, you have that problem. Of course if you have much money, you have a problem with that too, and

---

[44] Life pillar (Tib. *srog shing*): refers to the long, one-piece wooden pillar inserted as the axis of a Stūpa.
[45] Patrul Rinpoche (1808-81): an outstanding Dzogchen master, renowned for his scholarship and Bodhisattva conduct.

if you have nothing, you have the problem of how to survive. These are our constant worries.

Longchenpa's advice here is that it is better not to be interested in or give too much importance to these roles or people. This means we should not create many needs, but live in a simple way. Like that, we can integrate our life with every place and time.

THE NINTH WORD OF ADVICE

Carrying religious images, statues, offerings, scriptures, a stove
And all your requirements, you may go to a mountain hermitage;
Yet the paraphernalia meant to satisfy immediate needs are the source
of quarrels and problems.
Have no needs! This is my advice from the heart.

Some people, when they do a personal retreat, create many needs. They want a mandala, a statue, many books, articles for cooking and eating, and, naturally, a house to stay in. They busy themselves constantly with preparations thinking that such preparations are essential for a spiritual retreat. We can do the preparation and acquire what we need, but to be fixated on these commodities becomes a cause for quarrels and problems. Longchenpa advises us that it is better to be content with what one has: if the necessary conditions are present it is fine with us, if they are missing that is also fine.

THE TENTH WORD OF ADVICE

In these times of degeneration, you may scold
The unruly people around you, thinking it will benefit them;
Yet, doing this causes negative emotions.
Speak calmly! This is my advice from the heart.

The time of degeneration is the Kaliyuga,[46] the time in which we live. In this time we may be a teacher with many students who rely on us, or parents with many children that rely on our family. Sometimes, students and children are unruly, unwilling to accept advice not to engage in a certain negative activity. For example, they may like to drink alcohol to the point of inebriation, and this creates problems for their family, their group and so on.

When you as the teacher tell them not to drink because it is not good and that they should stop, they become angry; others like to smoke drugs and are attached to that. We, as teachers, know well that, as Padmasambhava explained, smoking drugs is a negative thing to do. If one smokes drugs one's clarity diminishes and one's energy, charged excessively, will be damaged. In particular, Guru Padmasambhava said that those who make use of drugs become passive, and becoming passive exposes one to all sorts of negativities.

It is obvious that smoking drugs is very negative, but if the teacher tells those who like to smoke that drugs are forbidden and that they should stop, or that if they insist on doing so, they should not come to his teaching, it is difficult for them to accept the advice. This is because, even though the teacher has a good intention, they are nervous and unruly. Moreover if, with good intentions, we scold them saying that they are doing something bad, just like parents do with their children, using strong admonishing words, they become angry and rebel against us.

Here, Longchenpa says that even if this is done for the benefit of others, one can create many problems, so it is much better to speak calmly with unruly people. If one wishes to make them understand, one should talk calmly to them at the appropriate time, when they are not nervous.

THE ELEVENTH WORD OF ADVICE

Without any selfish motive, you may tell people you love,

---

[46]   Sanskrit, 'age of strife', the last in the cycle of four Yugas or eras of this world as described in Indian scriptures.

With the intention of helping them, their mistakes;
Yet although what you say is true, your words are like a tumor in
their heart.
Speak gently! This is my advice from the heart.

With a good intention and without personal interest, we may tell others that what they are doing is wrong. Particularly, we may remind them on repeated occasions of the wrong they did. Although we are doing our best and are serious, yet to speak in that way repeatedly, instead of helping, makes the other person more and more tense.

Thus, Longchenpa says that it is better to speak with kind words. Instead of telling others their mistakes right away, suggest to them that avoiding a certain action could be more profitable, or explain that others who did the same suffered such and such a consequence, and so maybe it would be better not to do such things. We should thus communicate in a gentle way.

THE TWELFTH WORD OF ADVICE

With the thought of preserving the purity of the Teaching
You may engage in discussions, defending your opinion and refuting
that of others;
Yet in this way you create disturbing thoughts.
Remain silent! This is my advice from the heart.

People who become very learned often start to protect their own school or tradition. For example, a Sakyapa who writes books and commentaries explains how the teaching of Sakya Pandita is perfect and substantiates it as much as possible, but there are also those who do not agree with and refute Sakya Pandita's views, for example Tsongkhapa and the Gelugpa. Various polemical discussions with Sakya Pandita arose also in the Kagyü school. Knowing this, the Sakya scholar then proceeds to refute the views of Tsong-khapa and those of the Kagyüpa.

Many books have been written along this line, but such books are not found among the works of Longchenpa, and that is why Longchenpa gives this advice. For example, when I was young I studied in a Sakyapa college. In the Sakya school there was a very famous scholar called Korampa.[47] He was the author of many works, and among these, two are particularly well known: a commentary on the Madhyamaka and a commentary on the Abhisamayalamkara.[48] At the college I studied both works, because in the Sakya school they are considered to be very important. One of these works is entitled *Dispelling the Bad Views*.[49] I studied this book twice.

In this work, Korampa negates the Gelug point of view and the point of view of other schools as well. When he refutes Tsongkhapa, because of the importance Tsongkhapa had for the Gelug, he proceeds in a methodical refutation, stating his first point, second point, and so forth. The book is full of numbers of points, though I do not remember exactly how many they are. Sometimes, Korampa says, 'Tsongkhapa stated...' or, 'Someone said...' or he mentions one of Tsongkhapa's works, *The Gold Garland*.[50] I never studied this work by Tsongkhapa but I am familiar with Tsongkhapa's views and how these are refuted by Korampa. When I studied this book for the first time, I really thought that Tsongkhapa's points of views were incorrect. Korampa's refutation seemed very convincing. This is just an example, but in all schools, there are many such discussions.

In the Sakya, Gelug and modern Bönpo schools the monks are always engaging in debate, with the typical hand-clapping gestures and so on. When questioned about this method they reply that it is a dialectic discussion which serves the purpose of learning and verifying if the teaching is pure or not. Their idea is that if there is something wrong they negate it.

---

[47] Korampa (1429-1489) was a renowned Sakya philosopher.

[48] The *Abhisamayālamkāra* or *Ornament of Clear Realization* is a major work of the Mahāyāna tradition attributed to Maitreya. It is considered a commentary to hidden points of the *Prajñāpāramitāsūtra*.

[49] Tib. *lTa ba ngan bsel*.

[50] Tib. *gSer phreng*.

But Longchenpa says that even if they think they are maintaining the purity of the teaching, in reality, such discussions develop tensions and emotions. In fact, such discussions start peacefully at the beginning but often, after a while, the participants become charged and at times, really angry. Here, Longchenpa advises us that it is better to remain in silence.

THE THIRTEENTH WORD OF ADVICE

You may honor in a sectarian way

Your master, your lineage of teaching and your philosophical school;

Yet to praise oneself and despise others is a cause for attachment and anger.

Give this attitude up! This is my advice from the heart.

To honor them, some people say that their masters, and the lineage of the teaching and philosophical school they belong to, are much better and more important than others. In reality, this way of honoring leads to separation, limitation and sectarianism. Even if we think we do this for the benefit of the teaching, it actually yields the opposite result. In fact, to praise one's side and despise the other side is a cause of increased attachment and anger. Here Longchenpa advises us that it is better to leave this attitude aside.

Real Dzogchen practitioners always follow Longchenpa's advice: not interested in philosophical schools, they just pay respect to them. Respect is due not only to all traditions and schools, but also to all sentient beings. If there are ten persons, and among them some are scholars and others are stupid, that does not matter; all ten have their own dimension which is different and it is important to respect them all. To have respect does not mean to fall into some kind of limitation. For example, I have no idea—I really don't know—to which school or tradition I belong. In Tibet, there are four major Buddhist schools as well as the Bönpo school. Followers of the teaching, in Tibet, always have the idea that they belong to one or another of these schools. When I was small, I lived in a Sakya monastery and later I entered a Sakya College where I studied for five years. Because I had this opportunity, I studied the Sakya more than other traditions. Although the college was Sakyapa, our teacher had no limitations.[51] My interest, however, was focused on the Dzogchen teaching which is found chiefly among the Nyingma. Most of the Dzogchen masters are found in the Nyingma school, some also in the Kagyü school. Moreover, as a small child I was recognized as an incarnation belonging to the Kagyü school. So I have no idea if I am Kagyüpa, Sakyapa or Nyingmapa. I do not feel Gelugpa, not because I have a grudge against the Gelugpa but because I never had any contact with that school, while I did have interrelations with the other schools.

Years ago I was invited to a conference of Tulkus, or incarnate Lamas, in India.[52] I sent a message that I needed to oversee several examinations at my university and that I was not able to go. Later, I received another letter of invitation from the Dalai Lama. I thought I had better go because it would not have been appropriate to refuse. Thus I went to the conference with two of my students. The conference was to take place in Benares and when we arrived there we saw countless monks from all traditions. The conference organization had arranged for my accomodations but we did not know where the lodgings were. We asked a monk where the office of the conference organizers was. He showed us an office. We went there, and found that it was the reception office for Gelug Tulkus. There, a monk asked me which tradition I belonged to. When I told him that I did not know, he was very surprised. I asked him to check to see to which school Namkhai Norbu had been assigned. They offered us tea and they went to check in the offices of the other schools, Kagyü, Sakya and Nyingma. Finally, they found out I had

---

[51] The College teacher of Chögyal Namkhai Norbu was Khyenrab Chökyi Özer (1889-1960s), scholar and practitioner, one of the best students of Dzogchen Zhenga Rinpoche (1871-1927).
[52] This conference took place in December 1988 in Sarnath, on the outskirts of Benares.

been assigned to the lodging of the Nyingma incarnations. We went there and naturally they prepared lodging, food, and everything.

The next day, the meeting started and I went to the meeting hall with a label on my jacket that read, 'Namkhai Norbu, Nyingmapa.' There I met Tulku Chime,[53] a Lama who lives in England. We know each other very well, and we greeted each other. Then, Tulku Chime looked at me and said, 'What happened? Have you become Nyingmapa!? You are supposed to be Kagyüpa.' That is just an example. If I had not accepted the label of Nyingmapa maybe I would not have been provided with lodging, food, and so forth.

The Dzogchen teaching is an important teaching in the Nyingma, Kagyü and Bönpo schools, where it is considered to be the essence of all teachings, but there is no such thing as a Dzogchen school or Dzogchen tradition. For this reason, Longchenpa says that it is better to avoid honoring in a sectarian manner.

THE FOURTEENTH WORD OF ADVICE

Having heard and analyzed different kinds of Teachings,

You may think that comprehending the faults of others is wisdom;

Yet this is precisely the cause for accumulating evil deeds for yourself.

Maintain pure vision! This is my advice from the heart.

When we study in a college or another institution, we learn to analyze. We carry out analyses on what is good or correct and what is bad or incorrect. Having developed this capacity from the standard position of what we consider correct, we negate what we deem incorrect. In this way, we feel we are developing our Prajna or discriminating knowledge. We write books and give teachings based on such analytical knowledge, and everyone considers us

---

[53] An important reincarnation of the Kagyüpa school, born in Eastern Tibet in 1941.

excellent scholars. Even if this seems positive, in reality, by repudiating the other side we accumulate much negative karma. Here, Longchenpa advises us that it is better we train in having pure vision. Even if we are not convinced it is so, we should think, 'How good this is', or, for example, we should recall that all sentient beings from the beginning possess the self-perfected state. This is called pure vision.

The Vajrayana comprises the developing and accomplishing stages with countless methods to learn and apply. If one has the capacity to apply those methods, one can follow that path, but in conclusion, the most important point is to have pure vision, as stated by the famous master Atisha[54] in the three kinds of advice he gave for all practitioners. What are these three? To be a Hinayana follower means to keep the prescribed vows. Even if one is not a monk, there are lay or upasaka vows—for example, the vow to abstain from alcohol. If one takes this vow and maintains it, one is a practitioner of only one vow. One can also maintain two, or three, or four vows. Thus, there are different levels of lay practitioner or upasaka, without the need to be a monk or nun. Monks and nuns have lower and higher vows; in any case, with the vow we receive, we control the body, voice and mind, and in that way we shun negative actions.

Atisha says that a Hinayana, Mahayana, Vajrayana or Dzogchen practitioner must also know what the essence of Hinayana is and maintain that knowledge. With regard to the Hinayana, Atisha said, 'Refrain from harming others, and from the causes which lead to harming others'. This means that, knowing the essence of the Hinayana is not to create problems for others, one refrains from harming others, by controlling one's own body, voice and mind. For example, if someone tells us a person is bad because he did something wrong, and we go to that person and tell him that, we are not

---

[54] Atīśa Dīpaṅkara Śrījñāna (980-1054) was a famous Bengali master who taught in Tibet for thirteen years on the invitation of Lha Lama Yeshe Ö and Changchub Ö, kings of Western Tibet. Atīśa played a fundamental role in the second diffusion of Buddhism in Tibet and, with his main disciple Dromtönpa, developed the Kadampa school.

controlling what our mouth says and we have created a problem because now that person has become tense. How do we refrain from this action? We refrain by knowing that speaking in such a way is negative, by being aware. Even if we feel like telling the other person, we know that it will create problems and thus refrain from doing so. In that way, we keep to the essence of the Hinayana teaching.

How does a Mahayana practitioner maintain the essence of the Mahayana teaching? Atisha says, 'Perform what brings benefit to others, and seek the causes which lead one to benefit others'. This means when there is something we can do or say in order to help others, we are always willing to do it. This is related to our intention; thus with our good intention we act for the benefit of others. Bringing such benefit represents the essence of the Mahayana teaching: this is Atisha's second piece of advice.

If we have received many Tantric teachings which imply a commitment to perform transformations and visualizations, maybe we cannot do all these kinds of practices. How should we stay true to the essence of the Vajrayana teaching? We stay true to the essence of the Vajrayana teaching by trying to cultivate pure vision. When we are in the midst of many people we should always consider them as Dakas and Dakinis, realized beings. If upon seeing our teacher doing something wrong, we think 'how can our teacher do something like that?' we create a problem with the commitment to our teacher. In this case, it is better always to maintain pure vision. Regardless of whether we see or hear anything wrong, we educate ourselves, thinking that all we see and hear are our thoughts tied to our limitations and that in reality our teacher is an enlightened being. If we train in pure vision in this way we can not have any problem with the teacher. For this reason, Atisha said that for Tantric practice one always needs to train in pure vision. Here, Longchenpa in his advice emphasizes the same point.

THE FIFTEENTH WORD OF ADVICE

Proffering mindless talk on emptiness and disregarding cause and effect,

You may think that non-action is the ultimate point of the Teaching;

Yet to abandon the two accumulations[55] will destroy the good fortune of spiritual practice.

Integrate them both! This is my advice from the heart.

Some people who have only an intellectual understanding think that emptiness is the real nature of everything and say, 'Everything is empty, so it does not matter whether we do good or bad'. Saying this, they disregard the relative level, the relationship between cause and effect. There are many people who have this attitude. Among the followers of Dzogchen many think that this teaching requires no limitations, and that they are free to do anything they like, and they actually live out that idea. However, this attitude amounts to disrespect toward the relationship of cause and effect. Why? We are not always in a state of emptiness; we simply have a knowledge of emptiness. We know with our intellect that everything is empty, but in reality, we eat and sleep and so on, and all these actions occur in the relative condition. In the relative condition we must give the proper consideration to the relationship between cause and effect. Disregarding that will bring many unwanted consequences for our future.

Moreover, in the Dzogchen teachings it is said that when one dwells in instant presence, in the continuation of that state, one does not need any effort nor any concepts. To apply effort or to harbor concepts at that time would be negative. For that reason, Dzogchen speaks of there being 'nothing to do' or 'non-action'.[56] This is different from thinking of oneself as a Dzogchen practitioner simply because one has an understanding that

---

[55] Tib. *tshogs gnyis*, the two accumulations of wisdom and of merit.
[56] Tib. *byar med.*

all is empty. That is just intellectual knowledge, and, on the pretext of that knowledge, believing that one is in a state of Dzogchen, one neglects the two accumulations of wisdom and merits.

Accumulation of merit means performing good actions—for example, cleaning the temple, placing flowers or lights before the statues of the buddhas, making various offerings, helping the poor people we meet. With these actions we accumulate merit.

Accumulation or increase of wisdom means, when time permits it, staying in a calm state or, if we have knowledge of our real nature, developing that knowledge. If we do not apply these two accumulations, our spiritual practice will not unfold in a perfect way. Thus, Longchenpa advises us that the relative condition and contemplation must not be separated but should go together. When we notice that we are not in a state of contemplation, we should try to make the best of the relative condition we are in.

THE SIXTEENTH WORD OF ADVICE

You may think that the path of another's body[57]

*That involves the descent of semen, related to the meaning of the third
initiation, will enhance your practice;*

*Yet through this material path many excellent yogins have been
deceived.*

Rely on the path of liberation! This is my advice from the heart.

This advice concerns the practices which use sensation as the method. Many are attracted to sexual practices, so they buy books such as the *Kamasutra*, Taoist manuals, or Kundalini booklets, and try to apply their contents. Sexual practices done in a proper way yield good opportunities for spiritual progress. However, the ensuing experiences are very much related to our physical body,

---

[57] The path of another's body (Tib. *gzhan lus lam*), as opposed to the path of liberation (*grol lam*), indicates Tantric sexual practices with a consort.

to the material level. If we are not well prepared or lack the capacity and we do not have a teacher nor precise instructions, we can encounter many problems instead of gaining benefit.

Some people say they do Kundalini practice, applying some sort of Kumbhaka, holding of the breath,[58] pulling up the lower energies, pressing down the upper ones, shifting them to the right and left, but in the end they only develop illnesses. The practices involving Kundalini and Prana energy should be done very precisely under the guidance of a teacher. In fact, the Prana should circulate only in certain of the many channels of our body. If the Prana starts to circulate in the wrong channels the person very soon acts abnormally or crazily.

For example, there are cases in which people report hearing someone talking to them, even if no one is around. It is their fantasy, yet if we say to them that it is just a fantasy and no one is talking to them, they still concretely hear the voices. This problem arises because prana starts to circulate in the wrong channels.

The only way to solve this problem is to co-ordinate the energy of the person, provided there is a possibility of doing that. Such co-ordination of prana energy is very important; otherwise, with the passing of months and years some real threat to the life of that person can arise. For these reasons one must be careful with this kind of practices.

As Longchenpa advises, it is much better if we try to direct our practice toward our real nature, instead of charging our energy and working with it.

THE SEVENTEENTH WORD OF ADVICE

To give initiations to unqualified people
And distribute sacred substances to the crowd

---

[58] The vase-like holding of the breath at the navel region—a method of prāṇayāma, through which the control of vital energy or prāṇa is achieved.

Is the cause of slander and breach of commitments.
Be serious! This is my advice from the heart.

To give initiations to unqualified people means to give initiations to those who have no desire or interest in receiving them. Initiation is not just a kind of blessing; it is an introduction to the path which involves commitments. In fact, during initiation the teacher introduces the student to the path, so that interested students can apply that path in order to attain total realization. However, nowadays, most people perceive public initiations such as the Kalachakra as a kind of blessing. In Tibet, forty or fifty years ago, nobody would have given the initiation of Kalachakra or another initiation of the higher tantras in public.

The first public initiation of Kalachakra was given by the Panchen Lama. This was not the Panchen Lama who died recently, but the famous contemporary of the thirteen Dalai Lama.[59] After some problems arose between the Panchen Lama and the central government of the Dalai Lama, the Panchen Lama escaped to Eastern Tibet and Mongolia. He was a very learned Lama, so he became very famous in these countries. In exile, he started to give the Kalachakra initiation repeatedly in public, to thousands and thousands of the faithful. Later the Dalai Lama also began to perform the Kalachakra initiation in public. Since it was the Panchen Lama who gave it first, no one considered it improper, and thus it became a sort of established standard. Following the example of the Dalai Lama, other important Lamas also bestow the Kalachakra initiation on the public, considering it a kind of blessing, or as a cause for establishing a good connection with the Vajrayana teachings for many people.

Moreover, to distribute sacred substances to everyone is deemed improper. A sacred substance, such as the *nyongdrol*,[60] creates a cause for liberation in those who taste it. For that purpose, *nyongdrol* can be given also to those

---

[59] Thubten Chökyi Nyima (1833-1937). The Panchen Lama is the second highest ranking Lama after the Dalai Lama in the Gelugpa sect of Tibetan Buddhism.
[60] *Myong grol*, a Tibetan word meaning 'liberation through tasting'.

who are not practitioners. But if, with the idea that such sacred substances are important and wishing to establish in others the cause of liberation, we go to the market and give it out to anyone or we insist that others taste it for their benefit, this is negative and should not be done. If we behave like that, people who have no faith will dislike it and speak badly about us. In addition, this creates a breach in one's commitments.

When necessary, one can give *nyongdrol* to those who are interested. For example, one can give *nyongdrol* secretly to one's own aged parents. This does not cause any problem because we are motivated by the good intention of benefiting them.

In brief, Longchenpa's advice here is to be serious and not to do things randomly; he advises us not to give initiations or distribute sacred substances in a public way indiscriminately, as this is negative for us.

THE EIGHTEENTH WORD OF ADVICE

You may think that wandering naked in public

And other peculiar behavior is the deliberate conduct of a yogin;

Yet this is the cause for worldly people to lose faith in the Teaching.

Be considerate! This is my advice from the heart.

Sometimes, people who have achieved a certain degree of spiritual experience want to show their realization as the Mahasiddhas did, behaving in strange ways. Also, many people like to imitate Drugpa Kunleg.[61] Drugpa Kunleg was a Mahasiddha, and his behavior never caused him any problems, but if we were to behave like him we would quickly end up in jail. That is the difference. That is why here Longchenpa says that to do strange things in

---

[61] Drugpa Kunleg ('Brug pa kun legs, 1455-1529) was a 'crazy yogin' of the Drugpa Kagyü school and a disciple of the second Gyalwang Drugpa. Drugpa Kunleg became famous for his outrageous behavior which exposed the hypocrisy of his contemporaries.

front of ordinary people, such as walking around naked, thinking this is conduct without limitations, is inappropriate.

It is true that when we learn the teaching we must overcome and break limitations. But limitations must first be overcome with our mind, not with our body. Once we have created the capacity to overcome limitations with our mind, there are ways to do that with physical actions too.

To behave without limitations is considered to be the attitude of the Mahasiddhas, or of one who has gone beyond limits. However, such actions may cause a strange feeling in those people who observe us, particularly if they consider us practitioners of the teaching. When, as practitioners, we show an eccentric or abnormal attitude, people lose the faith they have in the teaching and stop following it.

For this reason Longchenpa gave this advice which is particularly meaningful for practitioners, 'Behave in a correct way with undistracted presence and awareness'.

THE NINETEENTH WORD
OF ADVICE

With the desire to be the highest one in the place where you live,
You may develop a good attitude and become very learned;
Yet this is the cause for falling from an elevated status to the lowest
*   position.*
Be neither tight nor loose! This is my advice from the heart.

At times, we have many good qualities and enjoy the respect of others, and become famous. In these cases practitioners need really to be very aware. When we speak of the four demons, among them is the demon of superiority. This demon arises in our mind when we become famous or important and others respect us. At that time we feel superior to others. This can happen also when we are doing a little practice and we obtain a minor siddhi;[62] then we think that now we are almost Mahasiddhas, and thus the demon of superiority arises. Practitioners should be very careful of this demon.

Once my female teacher Ayu Khandro[63] explained to me how she did the practice and the attitude she maintained. She told me how with her friends and two other yogins, she traveled to many sacred places and at the end of her journey she arrived in Kathmandu, in Nepal. They were constantly practicing the Chöd,[64] and when they met people with illnesses and other problems, they performed the Chöd for them, and there were signs of the success of their practice. Before long, every day hundreds of people would come to ask them for Chöd rites. Although they intended to stay for a month or so in the area of the Bodhanat Stupa,[65] when more and more people came begging them for the Chöd rites, a yogin friend of Ayu Khandro said, 'We should go away quickly otherwise the demon of superiority will arise', and they left. This is just an example; sometimes we can have this problem.

Practitioners can be very earnest, and as their practice develops to some extent, or as they learn a little about the principle of the teaching and are able to give explanations to others, they may become famous and others ask them for instructions. At that point, these serious practitioners change attitude, and they start to be interested in being teachers and in having many students; the demon of superiority is now governing their mind. Thus, we must be careful and present.

[62] Siddhis are accomplishments acquired through the practice, generally classified as common and supreme powers. 'Common' refers to secondary achievements such as that of lengthening one's lifespan, while 'supreme' refers to total realization.
[63] Ayu Khandro Dorje Paldrön (1838-1953) was a yogini, disciple of Jamyang Khyentse Wangpo (1820-1892), Nyagla Padma Dündul (1816-72) and other famous masters.
[64] *gCod*, lit. 'cutting off', a practice developed by female teacher Machig Labdrön (1031-1129) to 'sever' the four demons: the material demon, the immaterial demon, the demon of self-complacency, and the demon of ego-fixation.
[65] The Bodhanat Stūpa, also known as Jarung Khashor, is an important sacred site in the Kathmandu valley of Nepal.

Longchenpa advises us that although we may have good ways of relating to others, a good attitude or be very learned, yet, if we are not governed by awareness these qualities will become the cause of falling from a higher to a lower position. Thus, we should always be present, instead of charging ourselves up and at times feeling fantastic, and at other times feeling depleted.

THE TWENTIETH WORD
OF ADVICE

Wherever you stay, in a city, monastery or mountain hermitage,

Do not seek close friends,

Befriend all with neither intimacy nor hostility.

Keep your independence! This is my advice from the heart.

Wherever we live, may it be a city, a retreat place or, a monastery where there are many other practitioners, we should not be excessively limited by considering some as close friends and others as not one's friends. It is important to become aware of this differentiation we make among people. Of course, if we know a person for a long time and meet that person often, we consider him or her as our friend.

When we meet that person, we are happy and that is normal. But, for example, when we hold meetings or spiritual retreats, friends get together and form a kind of group separated from the rest. This is a limitation, and it is not good. We should be open to communicate with anyone. I don't say we cannot have friends, we can have friends, but friends are just friends, while the rest of the people in the spiritual community who follow the teaching are Vajra brothers and sisters.

The relationship with our Vajra brothers and sisters is much more important than our relationships with friends, even more important than that of husband and wife. When we die, normal relationships end. Our relatives, who were very faithful and kind to us, now and then may bring us flowers to the cemetery, but we do not live in the cemetery and we do not need any flowers. In truth, to bring flowers to the cemetery is useless; we bring flowers only to satisfy ourselves, just as when visiting a temple one brings flowers as an offering to the Buddha.

The Buddha has no desire to have fragrant flowers, but the one who offers has this attachment, and that is why one makes such an offering. In the same way for dead people, it is much better that we chant an appropriate mantra or do a Guruyoga, dedicating the merits to the dead person; this could help. Although the dead person is not in the cemetery, he or she is still somewhere in the six realms of existence.[66]

The relationship with our Vajra brothers and sisters lasts till we attain total realization. When we die, the relationship with such brothers and sisters does not change. For that reason, we spiritual practitioners need to respect each other, instead of always being distracted by our relationships with our friends. When we hold our spiritual retreats I always notice that people give excessive importance to friends and do not remember the relation of Vajra brother and sister, which for practitioners is more important.

Here Longchenpa's advice for us is that we should not create a problem for anybody with whom we have a relationship, whether or not they are Vajra brothers or sisters. Knowing that every being has its own dimension, we should respect each one. In that way, we live with awareness and presence.

THE TWENTY-FIRST WORD OF ADVICE

Behaving like a hypocrite, you may honor impressively the faithful patrons

Who provide you with sustenance;

---

[66] The six categories of rebirth (Lokas) within the system of traditional Buddhist cosmology: Devas (gods), Asuras (demigods), Human beings, Animals, Pretas (hungry ghosts), Hell beings.

Yet to feign in order to please others is to bind oneself.

Apply the conduct of experiencing all equally as one taste! This is my advice from the heart.

In Tibet, people would pay respect, offer food and help in various ways to persons who dedicated themselves to spiritual practice or other virtuous activity.

I do not know whether the situation is still the same today. However, when I was living in Tibet, practitioners who renounced worldly existence and went to live in the mountains to engage in spiritual practice did not experience any difficulty, even if they had no provisions. As soon as the people of that area came to know that there was somebody in retreat in the mountains who needed food, the next day they would go in numbers to bring food and other offerings. People had faith in the teaching and respect for practitioners, and thus eased their lives.

But there are some practitioners who, when they become the object of respect and of offerings, change their attitude and start to pretend to be important Lamas. Whereas yesterday they donned worn clothes, today, using what has been offered them, they dress very elegantly. We must not change our attitude when others respect us. To adopt such an attitude becomes a factor conditioning oneself, and even if, before, we did not feel attachment to material things, now our attachment increases.

Here Longchenpa's advice is to consider everything, good and bad, to have the same flavor. What does this mean? When conditions are good we are happy, when they are not, we become upset. This is how we usually are. To equate everything, good and bad and so forth, as being of the same taste, is the opposite of our normal attitude. To acquire this new attitude is not easy, but if we really have knowledge of Dzogchen, we do not remain bound to time and to our mental condition, and it is always possible to apply the conduct of experiencing all, equally, as one flavor.[67]

---

[67] Tib. *ro snyoms spyod pa.*

In Dzogchen, when we learn the four contemplations,[68] first we learn how to enter and be in the calm state. In the calm state we discover that there is considerable movement of thoughts. In Tantrism and in Dzogchen, such movement is recognized as part of our condition. In a different way, the Sutric path always emphasizes the principle of emptiness. Sutra explanations are based on the two truths. Many of you have read Buddhist books which explain the two truths, and you may think that such explanations are those of Buddhism in general, but in fact they represent the Sutra system. In any case, the first of the two truths is the relative truth: that is, how we perceive and how we are in our relative condition. The real nature of the relative condition is emptiness: this is called absolute truth. The absolute truth has to be realized or, to put it in another way, one must dwell in the knowledge of the absolute truth, while the relative truth represented by the samsaric condition is viewed as negative.

For that reason there is the concept of Nirvana and ordinary Samsara. Samsara is to be discarded and Nirvana is to be obtained. Many have the idea that Nirvana is a sort of paradise; in any case, here we have the concept of two things, one good and one bad. 'Same taste' means that Samsara and Nirvana are not different. How do we enter into the knowledge of the same taste? We do so by first discovering that movement is part of our real nature. The Sutra teaching does not possess such knowledge; it lacks that. In Tantrism there is the discovery that movement is part of one's own real nature, and movement is not seen as a valueless thing to be abandoned. Emptiness and its movement, its energy, are both part of our real nature.

Thus, we cannot obtain realization only by being in emptiness. Emptiness alone is a kind of experience. In the direct introduction, for example, everything dissolves in oneself, and one feels the experience of emptiness, but

---

[68] The four contemplations of Dzogchen Semde: the calm state (Tib. *gnas pa*); the state beyond movement (*mi g.yo ba*), the insight (*lhag mthong*); the absolute sameness (*mnyam nyid*) or integration of the experience of the calm state with insight; and the self-perfected state of wisdom (*lhun grub*).

we cannot say that to experience emptiness is to be in our real nature. Our real nature is the inseparability of emptiness and movement or clarity.

When we apply the four contemplations, first we discover the calm state, then we discover movement. That state in Tibetan is called *miyowa,*[69] or beyond-movement. Although the term *miyowa* is also used in connection to contemplation in the Sutra system, the meaning is completely different. In Sutra, *miyowa* refers to the Buddha's contemplation which cannot be disturbed by anyone, not even by demons who gather around him to create obstacles. The Buddha does not move away from the state of contemplation; thus it is said the Buddha is in the state of *miyowa* contemplation. This, however, is not the meaning of *miyowa* as used in the Dzogchen teaching. *Yowa* is a Tibetan verb meaning to move, *mi* is a negation, thus 'without movement' or 'beyond movement'.

How does one enter in the state beyond movement? If there is movement and one notices that, one is still in the dualistic vision, because one feels that the observer is here and out there is movement. For example, when we are practicing the calm state, and a car arrives making noise, we become distracted by that noise. Although we are applying the practice we remain in dualistic vision: we are here and out there is a car making a noise, but if we integrate the noise there is no problem of this duality.

Integration means knowing that movement is part of oneself. The movement within oneself is no different from other types of movement. If we realize that, we are no longer in dualistic vision. By being in the movement, we are not observing or looking at the movement, and we have thus become the movement.

Between the movement and our real state there is no difference. Being in such a non-dual state affects integration, and movement no longer constitutes a problem. At that point, one can finally discover the meaning of 'same taste'

---

[69] Tib. *mi gyo ba,* the unchangeable state, undisturbed state, not moving. See previous note.

or the non-dual state. In fact to be in the state of instant presence is the only way to effect integration. Instant presence is beyond time and beyond limitations of mind. In that state we can discover that good and bad are concepts and that the experience of good and bad is related to our mind, not to our own real nature. This is very important to understand. Thus, here Longchenpa says that we should be in the knowledge of the same taste.

For example, in the Drugpa Kagyü, one of the Kagyüpa traditions,[70] there is a special method and teaching of the one taste called 'the six kinds of sameness of taste'. Why six? Because we have five senses whose contact with their respective objects determines perception, enjoyment and so on. In front of us we might see a pretty flower we like, or maybe something ugly we do not like: we are always making such distinctions. We should not always be distracted by vision.

When we are in the state of instant presence and we see things, we are not distracted by vision. If what we see is pleasant and we like it, we can enjoy it, and if we do not like it, we leave it. This poses no problem since we are not falling into dualistic vision. Integration occurs in this manner. It is the same with hearing: people like nice music that gives a feeling of happiness when heard, but if someone nearby makes a terrible noise, although, that noise is simply a sound, we do not like it. In this way, we are always conditioned by our mind and judgments. However, if we are in the state of instant presence we can integrate everything in a perfect way.

The last sameness of taste of the six concerns the mind. Mind is that which thinks, judges and creates constantly. Although it is difficult to apply the principle of the sameness of taste in relation to the mind, if one has developed the capacity to integrate the sense contact with its object, then one does the same with mind; it will not be difficult.

---

[70] The extraordinary Drugpa Kagyü tradition originated with Ling Repa Pema Dorje (1128-1188), a disciple of Phagmo Drugpa, an eminent student of Gampopa.

THE TWENTY-SECOND WORD OF ADVICE

The methods based on interdependence found in countless books about such matters as divination, astrology, medicine

Are cause for omniscient knowledge;

Yet becoming attached to various subjects will disrupt one's contemplation.

Reduce the subjects you study! This is my advice from the heart.

In our life, we can learn and apply many disciplines, such as astrology or medicine. These disciplines can also contribute to the development of our spiritual practice.

In fact, with some of these, we can benefit others. We should dedicate ourselves to one of them and try to gain a deeper knowledge of that subject. For example, if we are interested in medicine we should only learn medicine and then follow that profession, but people want to study everything and always read books and study various subjects.

Moreover, in our modern society people like to read novels, instead of reading useful books. They take a long novel and everyday for a month or so, spend much time reading it. When they have read it all, they do not need that book anymore. Then they find another one, and spend another month reading that; this is a useless activity. Such activities take up most of our time and keep us occupied, preventing us from practicing contemplation; thus Longchenpa's advice is to reduce what we study, so that it does not absorb all our time.

THE TWENTY-THIRD WORD OF ADVICE

When you live in a house, leave aside furnishing the house.

In the midst of solitude you may arrange to have all comforts;

Yet, this only consumes one's life in triviality.

Put off all these activities! This is my advice from the heart.

When we are living in a house, we always harbor the idea that our house is too small, and that we would like it bigger. Once we have enlarged the house, we do not like its color, and want to change it. We always think about making some change. Here, the house is just an example, but this attitude extends to everything we possess. For example, if we have a car, we feel that it is too small; we would like a bigger one. Having bought a bigger one, we are not satisfied, and desire a more comfortable and faster car. We constantly engage in such pursuits.

When we are interested in following a spiritual practice in a quiet place, we think that we should make our retreat cabin a little more comfortable. Instead of actually doing practice we are always concerned with pursuing external changes. These activities are not very meaningful nor useful, and in doing them one wastes one's time. One must not spend much time in such pursuits. For example, in the biography of Milarepa it is said that when he was going to fetch water his light cotton robe would always catch on a small bush that was growing below his cave. He thought of cutting the bush, so that he would no longer have that problem. But he never cut the bush, because every time he went to fetch water he did not want to waste his time. That is an example; it is important also. Thus, Longchenpa's advice here is not to engage in trivial work or activities that waste our precious time.

THE TWENTY-FOURTH WORD OF ADVICE

You may persevere in spiritual practice—learning and virtue

And thus some of your qualities may become remarkable;

Yet whatever you cling to will bind your mind.

Learn how to be free and without limitations! This is my advice from the heart.

We may become expert in spiritual practice doing everything in a dedicated and precise way or become learned by receiving a good education and developing good manners, yet, these are just partial qualities that can create attachment. For example, we might think that we are experts in a particular field and thus know it much better than others; with such thoughts we condition ourselves. Longchenpa's advice here is to remain free, without conditioning ourselves.

THE TWENTY-FIFTH WORD OF ADVICE

You may think that subduing those who are to be confronted, with various rites of black magic and protection,

Such as causing hail and thunderbolts to fall, is enlightened activity;

Yet to burn the mind of another being will cause you to be reborn in lower realms.

Keep a low profile! This is my advice from the heart.

In the countryside, local people may ask practitioners to perform rites for averting natural calamities or harm caused by other beings. For example there are rites for causing rain when there is drought or for stopping rain when floods destroy crops, or rites to send away wild animals that damage the fields. In the texts that contain the collection of action mantras we find hundreds of different mantras for such eliminating or accomplishing purposes.

When we have the capacity and knowledge of how to use these mantras, we may think that to apply the related actions or to perform black magic will benefit the local people. In reality, this upsets other beings, so it is always the cause of a negative outcome. Knowing this, we do not become overly interested in these activities.

For example, some people complain that their houses are always infested by ants; they don't know what to do, and wonder if there is a mantra to get rid of ants. Searching in the texts of the collection of mantras, one can certainly find the appropriate mantra, but it is not sufficient to receive the transmission of that mantra and recite it for a hundred or a thousand times in order to make it work: one needs to recite it for some months, but after some months what have you accomplished? Only a small result.

Thus, Longchenpa's advice here is not to spend much time in activities which only make us waste our time.

THE TWENTY-SIXTH WORD OF ADVICE

You may have collected many useful profound texts—philosophical scriptures,

Spoken advice, transcribed teachings,

Yet if you do not practice, at the time of death, books don't help.

Observe your mind! This is my advice from the heart.

In the past, in Tibet, it was difficult to acquire books. It was even difficult to find the textbooks for college studies. Nowadays, the situation is different: finding books is very easy, and all kinds of books are published and available. People can buy books and read them. Sometimes reading books is useful, but often it is meaningless, because even if we have books of spiritual advice or transcribed teachings of masters, or useful books with a profound meaning, we just read them and do not apply their content. In this, there is not much benefit; we cannot bring books with us when we die. Thus, we should apply their content in practice, not just read them.

Here Longchenpa's advice from the heart is that instead of collecting books, we should observe our own mind. To observe one's mind means to check what kind of intention we have and what kind of intention we project. In this way we discover the good and bad intentions we have. In particular, we observe our mind in order to discover our limitations. Learning Dzogchen is discovering our limitations and going beyond them. One name of the

Dzogchen teaching is 'being beyond any kind of limitation that tips to one side or the other'. If we live in a limited condition we are not in the real nature of Dzogchen.

THE TWENTY-SEVENTH WORD OF ADVICE

When you practice wholeheartedly, you may have meditative experiences, discuss them with others,

Write commentaries, and sing songs of realization.

Although these are manifestations of the practice, they will only increase thoughts.

Remain in the state beyond concepts! This is my advice from the heart.

When we dedidcate ourselves wholeheartedly to spiritual practice we can have many kinds of experiences, good and bad. If this happens, we must check with our teacher or another expert practitioner whether our experiences are correct or not, and good or not. All experiences or visions we may have are related to our *tsal* energy and occur when the secondary causes for the manifestation of our energy are present. Although we have the primordial potential, if the secondary causes are not there, experiences do not occur. For example, the mirror has the capacity to reflect any object, and it does so instantly when there is a secondary cause, such as an object in front of it. A mirror kept in a box does not reflect anything. That energy, which is the characteristic manifestation of our potentiality, is called *tsal* in Tibetan.

In which other ways can energy manifest? Energy can manifest as reflections in a mirror, when you consider primarily the capacity of the mirror, leaving aside the secondary causes of the reflections. Even in a small mirror, big mountains and vast landscapes can manifest. These images do not appear outside, but within the small dimension of the mirror. The distinct way of energy manifestation exemplified here is called *rolpa*. In any case, Longchenpa says that our experiences and visions are related to our *tsal* energy. When we have such experiences and visions we may want to write them down or compose poems or other writings, or feel like expressing them in songs, as Milarepa used to do. In this case we must be very aware. If we lack awareness, such experiences and visions become a cause for increasing thoughts. Some people can have such experiences or visions naturally even if they don't do any practice. This is possible because the primordial potentiality is present in each one of us. Moreover, sometimes the secondary causes can occur spontaneously and when they do occur, experiences arise. These persons often become attached to the experience, thinking that their visions of lights and so forth are wonderful, but when they think that, such visions immediately disappear and do not manifest again.

Not recognizing that such visions are a manifestation of one's own potentiality, one falls into dualistic vision and attachment. That is why, in the teaching, it is said that when we have such experiences it is very important not to fall into dualistic vision, because, if we do, although the experiences themselves are positive they become a cause for increasing thoughts.

If we follow thoughts we can't practice correctly. Thus, leaving aside our thoughts we do the visualization as indicated. The purpose of visualization is to re-educate the mind. If we only like to follow our own thoughts, why would we do visualization? To follow what arises in our mind is not meditation. We have followed thoughts for countless lives to no avail; now we don't need to do that anymore. Longchenpa's advice here is that knowing the problems thoughts present, we do not follow them, and we relax in our real nature.

THE TWENTY-EIGHTH WORD OF ADVICE

When thoughts arise, it is crucial that you look at them directly,

And when you have clearly seen mind's nature, it is essential to abide in it.

Although there is nothing to meditate upon, it is important to remain in meditation.

Maintain the undistracted state! This is my advice from the heart

Maintain the undistracted state! This is my advice from the heart. When a thought arises what should one do? It is not possible to block thoughts; trying to block thoughts will only multiply them.

Thus whatever thought arises, without blocking it, one instantly observes it face to face. If one does that, the thought disappears by itself. When another thought arises, one is immediately present and observes that, and it will disappear. This is an essential practice.

What should one do on witnessing the disappearance of a thought? One just remains and continues in that state, till another conditioning thought arises. When one becomes distracted as another thought arises, one notices the new thought. When you remain relaxed in that state, you also discover that there is nothing to meditate upon. The best meditation is when one does not meditate on anything.

The Kagyü and particularly Gampopa explain the practice of Maha-mudra, speaking about four yogas.[71] The last of these four yogas is called *gomme*, which means non-meditation. Non-meditation is the discovery that there is nothing to meditate on. When we speak of meditation it means that there is something to meditate on. When we find that there is nothing to meditate on, we should relax in that state; that is really the supreme meditation.

---

[71]   The four yogas of Mahāmudrā are: the one-pointed state (Tib. *rtse gcig*); beyond concepts (*spros bral*); one flavor (*ro gcig*); and non-meditation (*sgom med*).

In what could be the conclusion of his teaching, Longchenpa says that what is most important is not to be distracted, to be present and relax in that state.

THE TWENTY-NINTH WORD OF ADVICE

Within the knowledge of emptiness, act in accordance with the law of cause and effect,

And when you have understood the principle of non-action,

Keep the three commitments[72] and strive to benefit all beings with non-conceptual compassion.

Unite the two accumulations! This is my advice from the heart.

Once we have understood or have had experience of our real condition, which is emptiness, we do not abandon the principle of the relationship of cause and effect. The main teaching of the Buddha was about the relationship of cause and effect. As you know, the first teaching of the Buddha was on the Four Noble Truths. He began by teaching the truth of suffering, so that listeners had something concrete to relate to. Suffering is universal, experienced by all sentient beings; no one can negate the existence of suffering. Also, no sentient being likes suffering. If we do not like suffering we must discover its cause and since suffering is the effect of a cause, we cannot overcome suffering only by acting on the effect.

The Buddha explained that the accumulation of negative actions is the cause of suffering. Although the Buddha taught that in order to overcome suffering we must first discover its cause, we do not understand nor apply this principle in our life. Our attitude is the opposite of that: if we have a problem we fight and struggle with it.

---

[72] The three commitments (Tib. *sdom gsum*) related to Hinayāna, Mahāyāna and Vajrayāna or Tantra.

For example, in the countryside people may complain about poverty and other social problems. To overcome these problems they start a revolution and kill half of the population. After the revolution is complete, nothing has changed. This is because we have not reached the cause; we are only fighting the effect.

The Buddha taught this principle in ancient times, yet people have not followed it. Even Buddhists do not teach this principle well. They explain the Four Noble Truths elegantly with analysis and with fine words. The Buddha, instead, taught it in a very simple and concrete way. He asked people, 'Do you like suffering?' Everybody would say 'No'. No one objected to his question. If he had begun his teaching by presenting the nature of the mind as the main point, the many spiritual schools of that time would have started arguing with him, and he would not have been able to teach.

So the Buddha began by teaching on suffering, the most common experience. If one does not like suffering one must still discover its cause; that is why Buddha then explained the relationship between cause and effect. To discover the cause in itself is not sufficient: one needs to stop, modify, or change that cause. For that we have the noble truth of cessation.

Not everyone has the same capacity to stop the cause. To those who had more capacity, the Buddha taught in a higher and more direct way, but this high and direct teaching of the Buddha was not understood by all. To those who did not understand the direct path, he taught a long path; although this path requires traveling a long way it is better than having no path at all. Thus the Buddha gave different kinds of teachings that comprise the fourth noble truth, the noble truth of the path. These points are not difficult to understand.

Longchenpa's advice is not to forget the relationship of cause and effect. We are not always in a state of contemplation; when we find ourselves in the relative condition it is important to act in accordance with the principle of cause and effect. Moreover, if we understand the real sense of the teaching, we understand the principle of non-action, that there is nothing to do concretely. We dwell in the real sense and we don't emphasize physical activities and so forth.

This, however, does not mean that we disregard the three kinds of vows or commitments related to the Sutra, Tantra and Dzogchen. We Dzogchen practitioners do not need to be monks or nuns, yet by being in the knowledge of non-action, in the real sense, without emphasizing physical action, we also maintain and respect the three vows and work constantly for the benefit of all sentient beings.

We know the principle, we don't simply adhere to an artificial altruism. We know that countless beings suffer infinitely because they are ignorant of their real nature. Having such knowledge, we cannot remain indifferent and we are always ready to benefit others. That is why we do the dedication of merits at the end of our practice. To dedicate merit is to create a commitment to dedicate our practice to all sentient beings. We practice in order to gain total realization so that we can be of service to all sentient beings. We need this kind of compassion.

Sometimes, people remark to me that all Lamas and teachings emphasize compassion, while I do not speak much of it. They say I should teach more about compassion. But we need real, not artificial compassion. We can have real compassion only when we discover our real nature. We know how many sentient beings there are who are ignorant of that nature.

You may have seen videos of the Dalai Lama teaching. Once I saw a video in which he was teaching the Bodhisattvacaryavatara[73] in Karma Ling, France.[74] When he started his talk he said, 'There are infinite sentient beings suffering in samsara'. Thereafter he cried and, for a few seconds, he was unable to speak. His was not an artificial compassion: it was knowledge of

---

[73] *Bodhisattvacaryāvatāra*, the famous text of the Indian Siddha Śāntideva (8th century) which explains Bodhisattva conduct and which concludes with a chapter on wisdom.
[74] An important Kagyü center in Southern France.

and the feeling for the actual condition of beings. We need such compassion, permeated by knowledge and practice. That is real compassion.

In conclusion, Longchenpa's advice is to join the two accumulations, that is, doing our best in the accumulation of merit in the relative condition, and in the principal accumulation of wisdom through meditation, contemplation and Guruyoga.

THE THIRTIETH WORD OF ADVICE

I have followed many learned and realized masters and received many profound instructions,

I have seen a few profound Sutras and Tantras and also examined them a little;

Yet whilst knowing them, I do not apply them.

Alas! I'm just deceiving myself!

In these last verses of advice Longchenpa says that he followed many good, expert, realized teachers and that he received many different kinds of teachings, that he studied both Sutra and Tantra, and that sometimes he also applied them. He says that, although he knows this, he is left only with an intellectual knowledge devoid of practice and that when he discovers this, he feels very sad. For that reason he gave these thirty words of advice to himself.

COLOPHON

For myself and those like me, I have spoken these thirty words of advice from the heart.

Of course there are other people like Longchenpa who perhaps need such advice, for them too he gave these thirty words of advice.

Through the merit of this composition written with the desire to attain liberation,

May all beings be liberated from the wilderness of conditioned existence,
and be guided to the state of great bliss.

May I become a supreme son who walks in the footsteps of the Buddhas
of the three times, of their heirs and of the great ascetics.

With the good intention of benefiting others, Longchenpa composed these thirty words of advice. Now to conclude, Longchenpa expresses the wish that through this root of virtue all sentient beings may be liberated from transmigration and obtain the dimension of happiness. Particularly for himself, he wishes to follow in the footsteps of the Buddhas of the three times, and their heirs, the Bodhisattvas, all realized beings, and following the way they practiced, to become realized like them.

Thus impelled by a slight sense of the arising of renunciation, I,
Tsultrim Lodrö,[75] composed these Thirty Words of Advice from
the Heart.

This text was written by Tsultrim Lodrö, a name used by Longchenpa for many of the works he wrote as a young man. We can thus infer that Longchenpa wrote these verses of advice when he was still studying and becoming a good practitioner, prior to dwelling in mountain retreats.

I myself received the transmission of Longchenpa's collected writings from Kunga Palden,[76] a great Dzogchen practitioner, who was the teacher of one of my uncles.[77] From the same master, I also received other teachings,

---

[75] One of the names of Longchenpa—see note 37.

[76] Drubwang Rinpoche Kunga Palden (1878-1950).

[77] The maternal uncle of Chögyal Namkhai Norbu, Khyentse Chökyi Wangchug, (1910-1960s) was the reincarnation of Jamyang Chökyi Wangpo (1894-1909), himself a reincarnation of the great master Jamyang Khyentse Wangpo (1820-1892). A biography of Khyentse Chökyi Wangchug, written by Chögyal Namkhai Norbu, will be published by the Shang Shung Institute in 2009.

some belonging to the Nyingthig Yazhi,[78] prior to entering college. When one receives a transmission from a teacher it is important to know how the teacher himself received the transmission. One cannot transmit a teaching, regardless of how interesting it is, for which one has not received the transmission oneself.

[78] The *sNying thig ya bzhi*, a collection of Dzogchen scriptures, compiled and partly composed by Longchenpa. It contains the *Bla ma snying thig* or *The Heart Essence of Vimalamitra*; the *Bla ma yang thig* or *The Quintessence of the Master*; the *Mkah'gro snying thig* or *The Heart Essence of the Dakini*; the *Mkha'gro yang thig* or *The Quintessence of the Dakini*; and the *Zab mo yang thig* or *The Profound Quintessence*.

CONCLUDING ADVICE

How to Integrate the Practice in Daily Life

WHEN WE PARTICIPATE in a spiritual retreat we listen, learn and do practice, but when the spiritual retreat ends we return home where we have many duties to attend to. Even if in the retreat we learned some practices, it is not easy to apply them afterwards: that is our concrete life. For a practitioner it is important to be aware and present in this concrete life; one must not live in fantasy. Some people can do practice when they want, but most people don't have such opportunities; they have many things to do, for example their jobs, and so they may think that their duty does not allow them any chance to practice at all. In fact, as soon as a spiritual retreat ends, some people email me saying they cannot do any practice because they have no time. This is not true. We cannot say that we have no time to breathe, we are always breathing. If that is so, why don't we have the time to be present? To be present one does not need to go to a particular place, one does not need to sit down and do something. At any moment we can be aware, and we can train ourselves to be present.

To be present is a very important practice. Sometimes we also have the chance to do formal practice, in modern society: we always have Saturday and Sunday free. Only on some occasions do we need to visit friends or relatives for their birthdays and so forth, but in a month we have at least three weekends free. We are not always busy. If we don't give too much importance to other activities we can find the time to do some practice.

We need to concentrate so as to make the twenty-four hours of the day become practice. To practice an hour each day is good, but not sufficient for obtaining realization. For example, we do an hour a day of practice but there are still twenty-three hours in which we are distracted and accumulate many negative actions. How can we attain realization in this way? We need to integrate the twenty-four hours into our practice. For that, we don't need to escape from our life and go to the mountains and do twenty-four hours of practice a day like Milarepa did. It is not feasible. Most people have a family, children and a job. It would not be bad if, renouncing all these, one were to go to the mountains and attain total realization in a week, but that is difficult.

Many westerners feel very satisfied doing a three year retreat. There are various Dharma centers where one can do a retreat for three years, three months, three days, three hours. It sounds very nice, and people leave their family, children and job to do that retreat. If there was a guarantee that after three years one would become totally realized, it would be fine, but no one can guarantee that after three years one will no longer need a family, a house, a job. Three years is not a long time; it passes quickly. After three years one is more or less as one was before, but not exactly, since now one has no family, no job. What is one to do then? Some re-enter the three year retreat. I do not ask my students to do such a retreat, neither do I suggest that they not do a three year retreat. If one wants to, one can do it, though I am sure one will not be totally realized after three years; that we should know.

The most important thing is that we integrate the practice in our daily life. That is the purpose of the Dzogchen teaching. Fortunately we have such a teaching and if we learn Dzogchen well there is always a chance to integrate it in our daily life. If I were to teach Sutra, or Tantra, which has complicated development and accomplishing stages, I could not say one can integrate these in daily life, because it is not easy to do. Instead, in the Dzogchen teaching we have that opportunity.

How do you start to integrate? First, by not being distracted. Learn to be aware and present and integrate your situation with Guruyoga. Try to do Guruyoga many times during the day. To do Guruyoga you do not need a special place or time; however, it is important to start the day with Guruyoga. As soon as we awake in the morning, we try to remember Guruyoga. If one remembers to apply Guruyoga continuously, one can have total realization.

INDEX *of* TIBETAN TERMS *and* NAMES

Ayu Khandro	a yu mkha 'gro 76
Bardo	bar do 26, 58
Bönpo	bon po 65, 66, 67
bskyed rim	22
byar med	71
Changchub Ö	byang chub 'od 68
Chöd	gcod 57, 76
Chöpa	spyod pa 28, 80
Dalai Lama	dalai bla ma 66, 73, 93
'dre 'dul	50
Drogmi Lotsawa	'brog mi lo tsa va 20
Dromtönpa	'bron ston pa 68
Drugpa Kunleg	'brug pa kun legs 75
Gampopa	sgam po pa 78
Garab Dorje	dga' rab rdo rje 11, 33
Gelug	dge lugs 9, 20, 64, 65, 67
Gelugpa	dge lugs pa 63, 66, 73
Gommed	bsgom med 90
Gompa	sgom pa 28
grol lam	11, 71
grong chog	50
grub chen	22
gser phreng	64
gsung	18

Gyalwang Drugpa — rgyal dbang 'brug pa 75

Jamyang Chökyi Wangpo — 'jam dbyangs chos kyi dbang po 95

Jamyang Khyentse Wangpo — 'jam dbyangs mkhyen brtse'i dbang po 76, 95

'jig rten chos brgyad — 55

Kadag — ka dag 14

Kagyü — bka' brgyud 9, 20, 64, 66, 67, 75, 82, 90, 93

Kagyüpa — bka' brgyud pa 64, 66, 67

Khyenrab Chökyi Özer — mkhyen rab chos kyi 'od zer 66

Khyentse Chökyi Wangchug — mkhyen brtse chos kyi dbang phyug 95

Korampa — go rams pa 64

Kunga Palden — kun dga' dpal ldan 95

Longchenpa Trime Öser — klong chen pa dri med od zer 9

lam — 11, 71

Lama — bla ma 50, 51, 66, 67, 68, 73, 93

lhag mthong — 80

Lha Lama Yeshe Ö — lha bla ma ye shes 'od 68

Lhundrub — lhun grub 14, 80

Ling Repa Pema Dorje — gling ras pa pad ma rdo rje 82

longs sku — 12

lta ba ngan bsel — 64

lus — 18, 71

Marigpa — ma rig pa 15

Marpa Chökyi Lodrö — mar pa chos kyi blo sgros 9, 20

Milarepa — mi la ras pa 84, 88, 98

mdo — 11

Miyowa — mi g.yo ba 80, 81

mo — 95

Nepa — gnas pa 80

ngag	18
ngo bo	11
Nyingma	rnying ma 9, 13, 20, 21, 66, 67
Nyingmapa	rnying ma pa 66, 67
Nyingtam Sumchupa	snying gtam sun cu pa 47
Nyingthig Yazhi	snying thig ya bzhi 95
Nyongdrol	myong grol 74
Patrul Rinpoche	dpal sprul rin po che 60
Panchen Lama	pan chen bla ma 73
Phagmo Drugpa	phag mo 'brug pa 82
phung po lnga	13
phyag rgya chen po	22
rang bzhin	11
rang grol lam	11
rdo rje	13
rDo rje sems dpa'	31
rdzogs rim	22
Rigpa	rig pa 15, 87
Rolpa	rol pa 88
ro snyoms spyod pa	80
rtsa 'khor	22
rtse gcig	90
ru shan	87
Samye	bsam yas 46, 95
Sakya	sa skya 9, 20, 63, 64, 65, 66, 67
Sakyapa	sa skya pa 63, 64, 66
Sakya Pandita	sa skya pandita 9, 63, 64
sdom gsum	91
sgom med	90
sgyur lam	11

sku	12, 18, 67
spong lam	11
spros bral	90
Tulku	sprul sku 12
srog rlung	22
srog shing	60
theg pa dgu	13
Thigle	thig le 17
Thubten Chökyi Nyima	thub bstan chos kyi nyi ma 73
thugs	11, 18
thugs rje	11
Tsal	rtsal 88
tshogs gnyis	70
Tsongkhapa	tsong kha pa 9, 20, 63, 64
Tsultrim Lodrö	tshul khrims blo sgros 46, 95
Tulku Chime	sprul sku 'chi med 67
yid	18
Zhenga Rinpoche	gzhan dga' rin po che 66
gzhi	11

TIBETAN TEXT

༄༅། །ཀུན་མཁྱེན་རྒྱོང་ཆེན་རབ་འབྱམས་ཕྱིགས་སུ། །
སྡེངས་གཏམ་སུམ་ཅུ་པ།
བཞུགས་སོ།།

༄༅། །ཚེ་རབ་འཁྲིན་མ་མཁན་འབྲུལ་ཡེ་ཤེས་རྡོ་རྗེ་ལ་སྡིན་ཆེན་པས། །
ཕྱོགས་རྗེ་ཉིན་ཞེ་བདུན་ངེ་ཉི་ཇུ་རྒྱུ་མ་ལེགས་ཁབ་ཁབས། །ཁ་དལ་འབྲི་ཞིང་ད་
སྲུག་སུམ་ཅུ་གུ་སྐྱེ་མཛད་དཔའི། །སྐྱབས་གསུམ་མཆོག་གྱུར་རྒྱོབ་མཛད་དུ
མ་མེ་ཞབས་ལ་འདུད། །

།སྨོན་ལམ་སྒྲོབས་ཀྱིས་སྐྱབ་བཅུ་དག་པའི་རྗེས་འབྲང་ཡང་། །ངས་ཉིད་
མེ་བ་ཆེན་ནོ་ཆ་མེ་ཆོ་ཝེ་ཁྱོག་སོ་གཏུག །ངས་སྲོ་ཉི་སྒྲོད་ཝས་ར་རལ
ཡེ་སྒྱུ་གཱ་ནེ་འདག་ཞན་ལ་ང་མཐོ། །འདེ་ཕྱིར་ར་བྲོ་ངས་རྒྱུ་བ་སྐྱུ་འཁྱིར
སྲོང་གཏམ་སུམ་ཅུ་བ་གད། །

གྱི་དེ་ སྒུར་ཚོ་ཁགས་ ཐབས་ཀྱིས་བ་འོ་རང་འ་བཟུགས་ནས་སོ། །མ་ཐུན་ཁྱེན
འཛོམ་པའི་དཔོན་ གཉི་འཛིན་པ་ལ་ཡང་། །ཆྱིང་པའི་གཱ་ཞི་དང་བད་ག་ལེ་མས་
ཞེས་པའི་རྒྱུ། །བཅིག་གཱ་ར་སྒྲོ་ད་གབོན་ས་སྲེང་གཏམ་ཡིན། །

སྲོང་ཚོག་ཉི་ཟླ་གས་སོའི་ འདུ་ལ་ལ་སོ་ག་ས་ཏྲྀ། །ཁྱོ་ཙ་ནཱ་སྒྲོ་ཝེ་ད་དུ་རབས་

ཁྱིམས་སྒྲུང་ཐུང་། །ཞེས་ནི་སྲིད་པར་བདག་གསོ་འདུད་ཀྱིས་ཉེན། །རང་
 སེམས་བདུལ་བགྱིས་ཤེས་སྟེ་རིག་ཆུས་ཡིན། །

དགུ་ལ་བོ་རྣམས་ལས་ཐབལ་ཆེན་བསྒྲུགས་ནས་ནི། །རྗེན་ཆེན་བཞེས་དངོ་
ལ་བབ་སྟེ་ལ་བོ་གས། །དགོ་ལ་བརྗེན་ནས་གཞན་ལྲིག་གསོག་པའི་རྒྱུ། །
རང་སེམས་བགོ་བ་ཤེས་སྟེ་རིག་ཆུས་ཡིན། །

རང་ཆེ་བདོ་ཕྱིར་གཞན་ལ་ཆོས་བ་དང་དང་། །གཡོ་ཐབས་ཆེན་པོས༌
མཆོག་དམན་འབྲི་ར་སྟོང་བ། །དགོ་བ་འརྗེན་སེམས་ཀྱི་རྒྱལ་སྲུ་བོ་
རྒྱུ། །བློ་སྲུང་བསྲུངས་པ་བཞོས་སྟེ་རིག་ཆུས་ཡིན།

ཆོ་དང་བུན་ལྲིང་གཡོ་སྒྱུ་ལ་སོགས་ཀྱིས། །ལོག་འཚོ་བས་ཟས་པའི་
ནོ་རྫས་བརྒྱ་འབུལ་ལང་། །ལོ་འདོ་དགོ་བཆོས་བརྒྱུད་དག་གི་རྒྱུ། །
ཞེན་ལོག་ཐོ་མ་པའི་ནོས་སྟེ་རིག་ཆུས་ཡིན།

གཉེན་དང་བར་པོ་ཐལ་ལྲི་ལ་སོགས་ཀྱིས། །གཞན་རྫོ་བསྲུམ་ལ་
འགྲོ་དོན་ཡིན་སྨ་ལ་ར། །ཁེ་ལ་བརྗེན་པའི་བྲི་བདོ་འབྱུང་བའི་རྒྱུ།

རེ་དོགས་མེད་པ་བོ་བོས་སྐྱེ་འགག་མ་ཡིན། །

མཐའ་རིས་ཡོ་ངས་སྐྲུ་ད་བོར་དང་བསོ་ད་རྣམས་དང་། །སྐྱེན་པའི་
གཏམ་བྱ་རྫམ་སྲིང་གཏུ་ཀྱུར་ཀྱང་། །རང་ཉིད་འཆི་ཚོ་ཐན་པ་གཡོ།
ཀྱང་མེད། །སྐྱབ་ལ་བརྫུན་པ་བོ་བོས་སྐྱེ་འགག་མ་ཡིན། །

གནུ་རེ་ལ་ཉེ་གནས་གཏོ་བོ་ལ་སོ་གགས་པ། །ཐབས་ཀ་སྒྱུ་བའི་སྲོ་གགས་ མིར་
མེན་བོར་ཀྱང་། །གནང་དུ་འཚོ་སྐྱེ་མེ་མས་འཁྲལ་ལ་སྲུང་བའི་ཀླུ། །
འདུ་འོ་བསྒྱུར་པ་བོ་བོས་སྐྱེ་འགག་མ་ཡིན།

ཊེ་ན་ལ་ཚོ་ད་པེ་ཚ་ཐབ་ཀ་ལ་སོ་གགས་པ། །ཅི་དགོས་ག་ནུ་རས་བོ་བོང་
འཁྲིམ་པ་ལ་ཡང་། །འཁྲལ་ལ་ འཚིམ་སྒྱི་སྲུག་ཀྱུས་ལ་ཚོ་ང་པ་ཀླུ། །
དགོས་མེད་བརྟེན་པ་བོ་བོས་སྐྱེ་འགག་མ་ཡིན།

སྒྲིག་ས་མའི་རྣམ་སུ་དྲུ་ནོ་ད་པ་བོ་རྣམས་པ། །རགན་བརྒྱ་ན་པ་ལ་སོག
ཐན་མེམས་ཡེན་མོ་ད་ཀྱང་། །དུ་ལ་བརྟེན་ན་ས་ཚེན་མོང་ས་སྐྱ་བ་ཀླུ། །
ནི་བར་སྐྱུ་བ་བོ་བོས་སྐྱེ་འགག་མ་ཡིན།

ཐན་པའི་སེ་མས་ཀྱིས་རང་བདོ་མེད་པའི་གཏུག། །བཊེ་བའི་མེ་ལ་
བཚོ་ནས་བཇོད་པ་ལ་ཡང་། །དྲང་པོ་ཡིན་ལ་བསྐྱེ་སྐྱན་འཐུག་པའི་ཀླུ།

སྐྱེ་བར་སྐྱོ་བ་བོ་བོས་སྙིང་གཏམ་ཡིན། །

རང་ཕྱོགས་སྐྱོབ་བིང་གཞན་ཕྱོགས་དགག་པའི་ཁྲུ། །བསྒྲུང་རང་བསྲུན་པའི་གནད་ཡིན་སྐྱམས་ལང་། །དེ་ལ་བརྟེན་ནས་ཉོན་མོངས་སྐྱེ་བའི་ཁྲུ། །སྐྱ་བཅད་བྱེ་བ་བོ་བོས་སྙིང་གཏམ་ཡིན། །

སྣུ་མ་དགའ་བཀུར་གྲུབ་མཐའ་ལ་སོགས་པ། །ཕྱོགས་རིས་ལ་འཛིན་ནས་ཏེ་ཡིན་སྐྱམས་ལང་། །རང་བསྟོད་གཞན་སྨྲ་ཆགས་སྡང་དགག་བོ་ཁྲུ། །ཐམས་ཅད་བསྐྱར་བ་བོ་བོས་སྙིང་གཏམ་ཡིན། །

ཕོམ་པར་ཆོས་ཀྱི་ནམ་དཔྱོད་པ་དཔྱངས་ས། །གཞན་སྐྱིན་རྟོ་གབ་ལ་ཤེས་རང་ཡིན་སྐྱམས་ལང་། །དེ་ལ་བརྟེན་ནས་རང་སྒྲིབ་གསོག་པའི་ཁྲུ། །ཀ་སྤྱང་སྐྱོང་བོས་སྙིང་གཏམ་ཡིན། །

སྤོར་སྣང་དུ་དཔོས་རྒྱུ་འབྲས་ཁྱད་བསད་དེ། །ཁྱར་མེད་ཚམས་ཀྱི་ལ་བར་ཐུག་ཡིན་སྐྱམས་ལང་། །ཚོགས་གཉིས་སྤྲང་པ་ཉམས་ལེན་སྐྱལ་བཅར། །རྒྱུ་འབྲས་སྣོམ་པ་བོ་བོས་སྙིང་གཏམ་ཡིན། །

གནས་པའི་དོན་དྲྱིག་ཡེ་རབ་པར་སོགས། ·········

གནན་ལུས་ལམ་སྒྱི་བོག་འདོན་ཡིན་རྣམ་ཡང་། །ཪག་བཙམ་ལམ་
གྱིས་སྦུག་ཆེན་བསྒུས་པ་ལ་ང་། །ཁྱིལ་ལམ་སྒྱིར་བོ་ནོ་བས་སྲིང་
གཏམ་ཡིན། །

སྐུལ་མེ་དག་ལ་དྲང་བ་སྤུར་སྦུ་ནི་པ་ཡང་། །སྒུ་བོའི་དྲས་སྲུ་དྲམ་
ཌ་ར་འཁྲིག་ལ་ནོ་གས། །ག་ནི་སྒུར་གའི་དྲང་ར་མ་ཆོག་ཉམས་པ་ནི་ཁྲུ།
བཚུན་འགོ་འདོན་ན་བོ་ནོ་བས་སྲིང་གཏམ་ཡིན།

སྒུ་བོའི་དྲས་སྲུ་ག་ཆེ་ར་རྒྱ་འཁྲིད་ལ་ནོ་གས། །ཧྱི་ཚི་ནི་སྒུ་ད་པ་བཙུ་
ཟུགས་ཡིན་རྣམ་ཡང་། །འཇིག་ཏེན་པ་ནམས་མ་དང་སྒྱི་བའི་ཁྲུ། །
བག་ཡོ་ང་ཚེན་པ་བོ་ནོ་བས་སྲིང་གཏམ་ཡིན།

ས་གྲུགས་འདོན་བ་དགེ་ཏེ་མཆོག་འདོད་ཕྱི། །བཚུན་དང་མ་འཁས་
ཤེ་ང་བ་ང་བོ་བས་སྤུ་ནབ་པ་ལ་ང་། །མཐོན་པོའི་ཚུ་ནས་དྲང་འཁས་ར་སྤུར་ནབ་འི་
ཁྲུ། །ཁང་སྒྱིད་མདོ་པ་བོ་ནོ་བས་སྲིང་གཏམ་ཡིན། །

སྒྱིང་དང་དགན་པ་རེ་ཐིད་ལ་ནོ་གས་ན། །གང་དང་སྒྱིད་གུང་སྦྱིས་མཇོའི་མི
འཚོ་ལ་ཞིན། །ནང་དང་འགྲོག་གུང་མི་མཇོ་མོ་འཛིན་པ། །རང་ཚིགས་
འཇིན་པ་ཁོ་བོ་བས་སྲིང་གཏམ་ཡིན། །

དཀྱུན་བོ་མོ་ན་འཚོ་བ་སྤུར་ལ་ནོ་གས། །བཆང་བོ་ར་བགུར་ནས་ཚུལ་
འཚོ་བས་སྒྱི་ད་པ་ཡང་།············

གཞན་ཕྱིར་བསྒྲུབ་ཕྱིར་བདག་ཉིད་འཆར་བའི་རྒྱུ། །རྡོ་རྗེ་ལྔས་སྒྲུབ་པ་བོ་བོས་
སྐྱེ་བ་ཆེམ་ཨིན།

བོ་རྗེ་ས་སྨྲན་ལོགས་ཨེ་ག་ལྟ་དཔག་མེད་ཀྱི། །ཉེན་འཚེལ་ཐབས་ཀུན་
རྣམས་ཉིན་རྒྱུ་ཨིན་ཀྱང་། །སྤུ་ཚོགས་ཚག་ས་ཕྱིར་བསམ་གཏན་གཉིག་
པའི་རྒྱུ། །ཤེས་རྒྱུ་བསྐྱངས་པ་བོ་བོས་སྐྱེ་གཆམ་ ཨིན། ༈

ནང་སྒྲོད་ཚོ་འབང་པའི་བགོད་སོགས་སྲང་། །དབེན་པ་བིའོ་རྡུ་ན་ཐུན་
ཚགས་སྒྲུབ་པ་ལང་། །ཁེན་ཆུང་རང་ལ་མེ་ཚོ་ཟེད་པའི་རྒྱུ། །ཀྲིད་ཉེན་བ་ཀོ་ལ་
བགོ་བོས་སྐྱེ་ང་གཆམ་ཨིན། །

མ་བས་དང་བཙུན་སོགས་སྒྲུབ་པ་ལ་བརྫུན་ཀྱུར་ཀྱང་། །ཕྱོགས་རིས་ཨེན་
ཆུ་ངལ་དུ་ཕྱིན་ཀྱུར་ཀྱང་། །གང་ཞིན་ཟ་ཨེས་བདག་རྒྱུད་འཆར་བའི་རྒྱུ། །
ཕྱོགས་མེད་རྱོལ་ཤེས་བགོ་བོས་ སྐྱེང་གཆམ་ཨིན། །

ཐོག་མེར་ལ་སོགས་གཏད་སྱུད་སྱུ་ཚོགས་ཚེས། །གཏུལ་ཁྱུ་ཚུལ་བ་
ཕྲིན་པས་ཨེན་སྣུམ་ལང་། །གཞན་རྒྱུད་ཤེག་ཆེར་རང་ཉེད་ངན་སྒོའི་
རྒྱུ། །དམན་ས་འཛིན་པ་བོ་བོས་སྐྱེང་གཆམ་ཨིན། །

གཞུང་དང་དབལ་གདམས་ནེན་ཕྱིས་ལ་སོགས་པ། །ནབ་མོ་ནིད་དབེ⋯⋯
དགོས་རྒྱུ་འཚེམས་ནན་ལན། །ཀྱམས་ཡིན་ལ་བྱུན་འཚོ་ཚོ་ད་ནེས་མི་ཐན།།
སོམས་ལ་སྤྱོན་ཟོར་ཟོས་སྐྱེ་ག་ཏུ་མ་ཡིན།

ཅེ་ག་ཅེ་ག་སྐྱན་ཚོ་ད་མས་དང་ནོ་བ་སྐྱུ་རང་། །བསྐྱན་བཆོས་ཅོམས་དཚ
ཉྲྲུ་དབྱང་ས་ལེན་པ་སོགས། །ཅ་ལ་སྱུང་ཡེ་ནཀྱུ་ད་རྣམ་ཐོག་འཐེལ
བ་དིཀྱུ། །བྱོ་བ་གཏྱོང་བ་ཟོར་ཟོས་སྐྱེ་ག་ཏུ་མ་ཡིན། །

རྣམ་ཐོག་སྐྱེས་ཚེ་ཅེར་སྐྱིས་སྐྱ་བ་ག་ཅེས། །སེམས་ཐག་ཆེན་ཚེ་ཐོག་ཏུ
བཞག་པ་ག་ཅེས། །སྐོ་མ་དུ་ལོན་དཀུང་སོག་དུ་ཝག་ལ་ག་ཅེས། །ཡིན་ས
མེ་ད་སྐོང་ས་ཟོར་ཟོས་སྐྱེ་ག་ཏུ་མ་ཡིན།

སྦོ་དེ་དང་ནས་རྒྱ་འབས་སྦོ་ད་དེ་ཅིང་། །ཐུར་མེ་ད་ཟོག་ས་ན་སྐོམ
ག་སམ་སྔུ་བ་དང་། །དམི་ག་ས་མེ་ད་སྐྱེ་ད་ཟེ་ས་འགྲོ་ལ་ཐན་བཚན་པ།
ཚོག་ས་ག་ཉེས་དཝུར་མེ་ད་ཟོར་ཟོས་སྐྱེ་ག་ཏུ་མ་ཡིན། །

མ་ཟེ་ས་སྒྲུ་བ་སྒྲ་མ་ལང་བ་སྐྱེ་ས་ག་དྲ་པ་ཟབ་བ་མོ་ནད་ཐོ་ས། །མ་ད་རྒྱུ་ཟབ
མོ་པ་ག་ནམ་ཟོན་ད་དུར་བེས་ནང་དུ་བ་ཏུ་ག་ས། །ཤེས་བ་ཟེན་མི་སྐྱོ་ད་ཅེ་ཁ
པ་ཟོེ་ས་ན་ད་བ་སྐྲུ་ས་པ། །

རང་རབ་བག་ཡོད་འི་ཆུལ་ལ་སྐྱེས་ག་ཆ་སྲོམ་ཙུ་ར་ཧར། །རེས་འབྱུར་ཡིད་
ཀྱིས་འདི་ན་རྩ་མས་དགོ་རེས་ར་བགོ་བ་ཀུ། །སྲིད་པའི་དགོན་པ་ལས་
བསྐལ་བ་རེ་ཆེན་ལ་བགོ་ན་རེ། །རྒས་གསུམ་རྒྱལ་རང་འེ་སྲས་ང་རྒོ་ཆེ་
རྣམས་གྱི། །རྗེས་སུ་སྐྱོད་པའི་རྣམ་ཅི་ཐུབ་བོ་ར་བ་དགའ་སྐུར་ཆེག །སྐྱིང་
ག་ཆག་སྲམ་ཙུ་བ་ནས་ཐུབ་བ་རེས་ཧར་ཧུབ་བ་ཐུང་རར་གྱི་སྐྱོན་བ་སྐྱལ་བ
ཆུ་ལ་ཞིམས་ཐོ་གོས་ཆེས་སྲར་བོ། །དགེའོ།། ༄།།

*Finito di stampare
dalle Grafiche Vieri - Roccastrada
nel mese di Gennaio 2009*